Make it in Cheesecloth

Hazel Todhunter

B T BATSFORD LTD   LONDON

Make it in Cheesecloth

CONTENTS

INTRODUCTION

A loosely-woven cotton fabric, cheesecloth was originally used, as its name suggests, to cover cheeses which were being stored and matured. Before the 'sixties it had never been considered a fashion fabric, yet today cheesecloth is one of the most popular materials used for young leisurewear. Its soft, casual look teams well with jeans and flounced skirts, or with T-shirts and summer tops, and complements any type of shoe fashion, from high heels to espadrilles.

Cheesecloth is a very versatile fabric: it conjures up pictures of pretty sundresses and smock tops edged with lace, yet it can also lend itself to an elegant sophisticated look for evening wear and special occasions. It can be used to make a host of small household items, such as napkins and small fabric drawstring bags (for holding pepper corns, coffee beans, rock salt and herbs, or larger items such as clothes pegs etc), as well as clothes and accessories, such as dresses, shirts, tunics, skirts, sun tops, caftans, scarves, headsquares, belts and soft jewellery.

It can be bought in a wide range of soft pastel colours or bright checks, stripes and patterns, and by adding frills, flounces, braids and couched motifs, or decorating it with shirring, top stitching, embroidery or dyeing a variety of effects can be produced from one basic shape. Being made of a natural rather than a man-made fibre, cheesecloth is comfortable to wear and easy to care for; it can be washed again and again without losing its freshness — and you do not even need to iron it unless you wish to.

This book has been written with the complete beginner in mind, and gives step-by-step instructions for making a whole range of garments and accessories. All the items are cut from simple rectangles of cloth, to be sewn by hand or machine, so there are no complicated measuring systems or dressmaker's patterns to cope with. All the styles are so quick to make up they can be finished in an evening, and they have been specially designed to fit all ages on a large/medium/small basis; the loosely flowing shapes, elasticated tops and wraparound waistbands will provide a comfortable fit whatever your size.

So for those who have never before considered dressmaking with cheesecloth, yet would like to create something original, this book will provide all the information necessary on treating, preparing and working the fabric. It will also help those on a budget to achieve the maximum effect in fashion with a minimum of effort and cost.

TOOLS AND EQUIPMENT

Always endeavour to look after your tools, keep them together in a box, basket or other suitable container — and try not to let anyone borrow them. In the end this simple rule saves time and temper as you search, yet again, for your sewing scissors or your tape measure.

Chalk

This is used for marking out cheesecloth. Tailor's chalk is the most convenient as it has a sharp edge for drawing lines. Use white chalk on coloured cheesecloth and coloured chalk on white or light coloured fabric. Keep chalk in a small polythene bag with a self-seal strip so that it cannot crumble over the contents of your work-basket. Alternatively, use an ordinary plastic bag, knotted or sealed with an elastic band, or a folded envelope.

Dressmaker's carbon paper

This is used to transfer designs to the cheesecloth. Ordinary carbon paper smudges too easily, but if you cannot obtain dressmaker's carbon, you can, using extra care, use sheets of ordinary carbon paper which have had most of their carbon rubbed off onto newspaper. To use the paper, you will need the following items:

    a board slightly larger than the cheesecloth
    drawing pins or cellophane tape
    paper for a mask
    dressmaker's carbon
    paper for the design
    ball-point pen or pencil

Pin or tape the cheesecloth to a board or other flat surface. Make sure that it is right side up. Cut a hole in the paper, making it slightly larger than the design you are transferring. Place this mask over the cheesecloth, then place the carbon paper on top, carbon (shiny) side down. Finally put your design on top and pin through all the layers to hold them in place (diagram 1).

Carefully go over the lines of the design using a pen or pencil. (A fibretip pen does not leave any impression and so should not be used.) When you

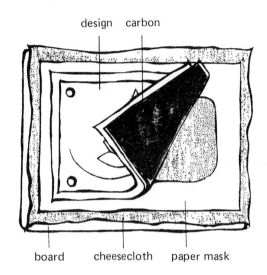

design   carbon

board   cheesecloth   paper mask

Diagram 1   *Using dressmaker's carbon*

have traced the complete design, lift up one corner and check that the design shows up clearly; if not, go over the design once again. Lift off the carbon, mask and design.

This process may seem unnecessarily complicated — but masking the cheesecloth prevents carbon rubbing off where you rest your hands. Such marks are always easier to get onto the fabric than off.

Embroidery pencil

This is an alternative to dressmaker's carbon. You can obtain an embroidery pencil from a large department store, from a specialist handicraft shop, or from some large fabric stores.

To use the pencil, trace the design to be transferred, turn over the tracing, and draw over the lines of the reversed design using the embroidery pencil. Position the tracing over the cheesecloth, pencil side up. Transfer the design by pressing with a hot iron.

It is important to keep the embroidery pencil sharp otherwise it will produce smudgy lines which are difficult to cover.

Fabric adhesive

Use a latex or plastic adhesive that is specially made for fabric, such as Copydex (UK) or Elmer's Glue-All (USA). Always use it sparingly, otherwise it will mark the fabric if it comes through to the right side and in time will turn brown. It will not come off.

Apply the adhesive with the end of a spent match or a cocktail stick. Wait for it to become tacky — but not dry — then press the two surfaces together. They will stick as soon as they touch, so make sure that they are correctly positioned.

If you do not allow the adhesive to dry a little before pressing the surfaces together, the pressure of your fingers will force the adhesive through to the right side of the cheesecloth.

Iron

An essential to good dressmaking is pressing, and for this you will need an iron and a pressing cloth; a clean tea towel will suffice. (If you have a steam iron you will not need a cloth.)

An ironing board is very useful, but not essential; you can use an old blanket to protect a table. Although it adds to the clutter of dressmaking, I prefer to set up my ironing board and iron so that I am not tempted to skip out the pressing stage.

Needles

The best way to avoid losing needles is to keep them in their packets, or in a needlecase. Never put needles (even temporarily) into the nearest piece of upholstery, or the edge of your skirt: you may know where the needle is, but nobody else will. Needles embedded in your hand are very painful, and can be dangerous if they snap off.

Choose a needle type and length that suits you, but take care to pick the right size. Too thick a needle leaves unsightly holes and easily unthreads itself, too fine a needle makes threading and sewing unnecessarily difficult. Always thread your needle using the thread end which hangs from the reel. This prevents the thread twisting and knots forming as you work. Self-threading needles are available, but I find that occasionally they cause the thread to snap.

If you are using a sewing machine make sure that you change your needle to suit the fabric. You may find a ball-point needle the most suitable for sewing lightweight cheesecloth.

Needle threader

This is a very simple tool (diagram 2), often supplied with packets of needles, and one which many people would not be without. It does save time and is easy to use. Simply push the diamond-shaped wire through the eye of the needle, pass the thread through the wire, then pull the wire back through the needle, taking the thread with it.

Diagram 2   *Needle threader*

Pins

Use long pins with cheesecloth, as short pins tend to fall out. Keep your pins in a tin, small box or screw-top jar. A piece of polyurethane foam (or underfelt) stuck to the top becomes a pin cushion. Keep the anti-rust paper from the pin box or a few grains of rice with the pins; it will prevent them from rusting. As with needles, do not leave pins lying around.

Scissors

Sharp scissors are essential for sewing. Blunt scissors make cutting out difficult and tedious. They cause bumps on your fingers and fray the edge of the fabric, making it unpleasant to sew — and spoiling the finished result.

You will need a pair of large cutting-out scissors, not necessarily large dressmaking shears, unless you intend to cut very heavy fabrics, and a smaller pair of sharp pointed scissors for cutting threads and trimming fabric. It is worth spending time and effort to acquire scissors with a grip that really fits your hand comfortably. There are several sorts of moulded grip handles available, not all suitable for all hands, so it is a good idea to try out several pairs before buying. Take along a spare piece of fabric to try them on.

If you are left-handed some large department stores and specialist shops now stock left-handed scissors. Should you not be able to find scissors that fit your hand comfortably or if you already have an unsuitable pair, you can improve their fit by wrapping cotton wool or knitting wool round the handles.

If all this seems a vast amount of fuss for just one pair of scissors, take heart, they should last for years — provided they are not lent out for non-dressmaking purposes, such as cutting flowers, string or opening food packets. The same holds true of cutting paper. Keep a separate pair of household scissors handy for making patterns or anything else which involves cutting paper.

Sewing machine
A sewing machine is very useful, but not essential. It can be quicker to sew a seam by hand than to set up and thread your machine. Also, you can take hand sewing out and about with you and continue with it in spare moments. If you do have a sewing machine, make sure that you clean it regularly. Remove any build-up of fluff frequently, and check that the needle is not blunt or bent.

Tape measure
This is used to check measurements and for marking out cheesecloth. An old tape measure may have stretched and may therefore be inaccurate. Treat yourself to a new one, the small expenditure on worthwhile equipment will do wonders for morale.

Thimble
It sounds so old-fashioned, but using a thimble still makes good sense if you intend to do more than an occasional piece of hand sewing or embroidery. The idea is to prevent sore fingers, so do buy a thimble which fits your middle finger closely and does not rub. Remember that you can bend a metal thimble if necessary; this is not possible with the plastic type and I know few, if any, people with circular finger tips. If, after trying, you are unable to sew using a thimble, sticking plaster wrapped around your finger tip will give considerable protection.

Thread
Logically, one should use a natural thread with a natural fabric, ie a cotton thread for cheesecloth.

However, cheesecloth is such a stretchy fabric that cotton often snaps. A synthetic thread (such as Drima) does stretch with the fabric, and is quite suitable for use on cheesecloth.

Tacking thread
You probably will not need to buy special thread for tacking — you can use any odd reels that have accumulated about the house. Choose a contrast colour that shows up clearly. The whole point is that you should not confuse tacking-thread with that used for the actual sewing — which is why tacking-thread was traditionally red. Imagine removing the wrong thread by mistake and having to sew an entire hem or seam again.

Stitch marker
A stitch marker is a wooden-handled wheel which marks off the required number of stitches to the centimetre (inch). This small tool is not essential, but can be useful in marking off the length of each stitch on the fabric before hand sewing so that the result is even, and helps give a professional finish to the work.

Tracing paper
It is not necessary to buy special tracing paper, you can use kitchen greaseproof, or any other thin paper.

Work baskets
You can buy beautifully trimmed work baskets from most large stores, but they are expensive, and there are many alternatives. A cutlery tray has divisions to keep items separate, so does a shoe tidy — and if it is of clear plastic you can see at a glance where things are hiding. A household tidy, designed to hold washing-up liquid, scouring powder and the like, has the advantage of a handle. You could use a plain wicker basket or rattan box, but a bread basket is very cheap and easily available — so are prettily decorated biscuit and confectionery tins. Simply ensure that the container is large enough to contain all the smaller items of equipment.

BASIC SEWING TECHNIQUES

Cutting out

When cutting out, being able to spread the cheesecloth out is essential and finding sufficient space can be a problem. A table is convenient for small things, but for large articles a clean floor is probably the best, if not the most obvious choice. Make sure that no one is going to walk on your chosen piece of floor while you are working, then spread out the cheesecloth. If it is a tiled or wooden floor use small pieces of cellophane tape to hold the fabric in place. If it is carpeted, use pins — but make sure you remove them *all* when you have finished. Also, do not attempt to cut out on a shag pile carpet — unless you want it shorn.

Before you start cutting out make sure that you understand the instructions. Then, using the relevant diagram as a guide, mark out the cheesecloth following the cutting out instructions. One way of marking out shapes is to use the blunt end of a needle or a pin to pull out a thread (diagram 3). Alternatively, you can use tailor's chalk.

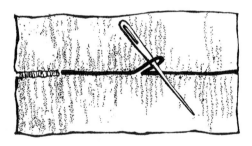

Diagram 3   *Pulling a thread*

On the checked or striped cheesecloth use the woven pattern as a guide, although you will still have to pull thread across stripes. Use your large scissors to cut out. If you have marked the pieces by pulling threads you can remove the fabric from the floor and cut out on the table or your lap. As soon as you have cut out each piece, label it, either by writing on it using tailor's chalk, or by pinning on a written label. Be consistent and label the right or the wrong side of each piece.

Tacking

Although experienced dressmakers often omit tacking, if you are just beginning to sew, it is advisable to tack. In the long term it saves time, and makes the rest of the sewing and fitting so much easier. Tacking is essential if you have to match stripes or checks.

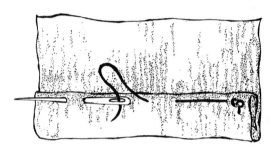

Diagram 4   *Tacking*

Use a colour that shows up against the cheesecloth. Thread the needle, and make a knot at the end of the thread by laying the end of the thread over your index finger, laying the needle on top of that and holding it in place with your thumb; wind the thread three times round the needle, then slide this wound thread down the needle and down the rest of the thread with finger and thumb until it forms a knot at the end. Insert the needle close to the edge of the hem or seam, then use large running stitches to hold the fabric in place. Avoid pulling the stitches tight or they will snap when you stretch the seam whilst sewing. Fasten off with two or three back stitches. To remove, cut the thread and pull out the tacking using the blunt end of a needle or pin.

Seams

No matter how strong the fabric, if seams are poorly sewn your garment will quickly fall apart. To avoid this, make sure that all thread ends are securely fastened on and off. It is preferable to fasten on with several small back stitches, rather than a knot

— knots always pull through in time. Similarly, fasten off securely with several small back stitches. If you are using a machine, pull threads behind the presser foot before you start, and leave sufficient thread at the end of the seam to sew several knots. Knot both ends securely. This sounds tedious and boring — but well-made clothes should seldom need running repairs, accidents excepted.

To sew the seam, use machine stitch, running stitch (diagram 5) or back stitch (diagram 6).

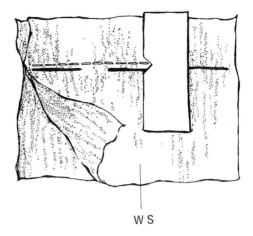

W S

Diagram 7   *Flat seam showing card guide*

Diagram 5   *Running stitch*

If you are using a sewing machine, your machine may have a sewing guide (diagram 8) marked on the metal base plate (ie the plate that the needle goes through). If there is not one marked on your particular machine, measure about 1.5 cm (⅝in) away from the hole that the needle goes through, and mark the width of the seam with coloured adhesive tape.

Running stitch is quicker to work than back stitch, but not nearly so strong. If the thread snaps, the whole seam quickly comes undone, whereas a back stitch seam will hold. This is an important consideration when using a fabric as stretchy as cheesecloth.

Diagram 6   *Back stitch*

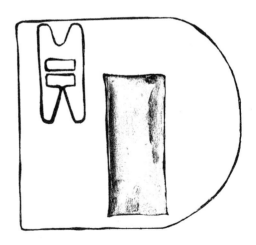

An alternative, which combines speed of work and strength, is to work running stitches with a back stitch every fourth or fifth stitch. Whether sewing by hand or by machine, stretch the fabric as you stitch.

Diagram 8   *Needle plate guide*

Flat seam   Put the right sides of the fabric together and pin at intervals. If you are using a checked or striped fabric, now is the time to make sure that the pattern matches. Tack along the seam and remove the pins. Use a piece of card to make a sewing guide (diagram 7). The notch should be cut about 1.5 cm (⅝in) in from the edge, to indicate the depth of the seam.

Remove the tacking and press the seam before continuing. If the edges that have been joined are not selvedge edges (ie the firm, finished edge of the material, indicated in the diagrams by a zigzag line), they will now have to be neatened.

French seam   This may seem rather formidable, but with practice it becomes quite easy, and can take less time than sewing and neatening a flat seam.

To work the seam, put the *wrong sides* of the fabric together. Make sure that stripes or checks match, then pin and tack as for a flat seam (diagram 9). Sew the seam 0.5 cm (¼ in) from the edge, remembering to stretch the cheesecloth as you sew. Carefully trim the seam allowance to about half its width, using sharp scissors. Remove the tacking and press.

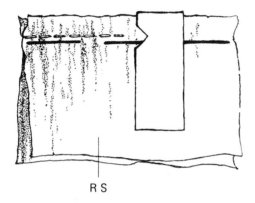

R S

Diagram 9   *French seam (first stage)*

Fold the cheesecloth so that the right sides are together. Tack, making sure that all the raw edges are enclosed (diagram 10). Work a second seam 1 cm (⅜ in) from the folded edge. Once again, stretch the fabric as you sew. Give a final press after removing the tacking.

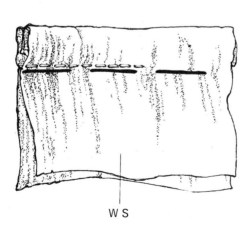

W S

Diagram 10   *French seam (second stage)*

Neatening raw edges

Unless a flat seam joins two selvedges you will have to neaten the raw edges to prevent the fabric from fraying away. There are several ways of doing this.
Using pinking shears   This is the simplest, and quickest method (diagram 11), providing that you have a pair of pinking shears (heavy scissors with blades shaped to form a saw-toothed edge).

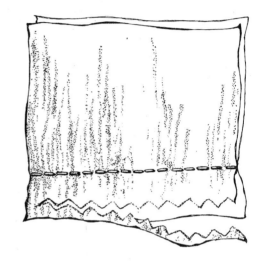

Diagram 11   *Neatening seam allowance with pinking shears*

Oversewing   This stitch can be used very quickly to neaten an edge (diagram 12); it can also be used to join two neatened edges, or to make eyelets (ie to strengthen the fabric around a punched hole).

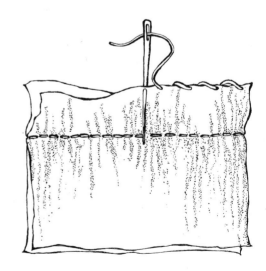

Diagram 12   *Neatening seam allowance by oversewing*

Top stitching Turn under 0.5 cm (¼ in) on each seam allowance, and hold in place with running stitch or machine stitching (diagram 13).

Diagram 13 *Neatening seam allowance by top stitching*

Machine stitching You can only use this method if you have a zigzag sewing machine. Set the zigzag to the maximum stitch width and a medium stitch length. Stitch along the length of the seam allowance (diagram 14).

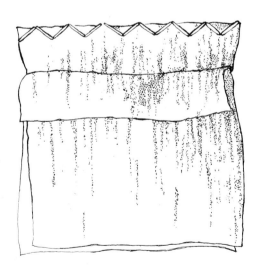

Diagram 14 *Neatening seam allowance by machine stitching*

Hems

A neat, straight hem can be extremely difficult to sew. The secret is not to use tiny stitches, but to make sure that the stitches, whatever their size, are regular in length and spacing.

Fold the hem with the wrong sides of the fabric towards you. Turn down 1 cm (⅜in) and hold it between one thumb and forefinger. Use your other thumb and forefinger to crease the fold into place. Turn the second fold of the hem in the same way, but make it the width given in the instructions. Make sure that any loose threads are enclosed in the folds. Pin into place (diagram 15), then tack and press.

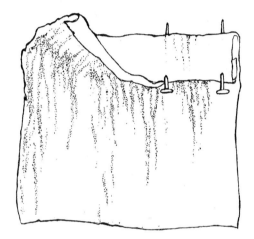

Diagram 15 *Turning a hem*

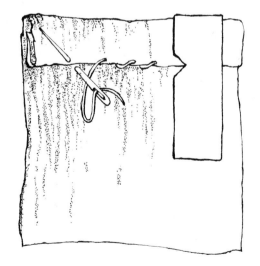

Diagram 16 *Stitching the hem with a hem guide*

Following diagram 16 stitch the hem into place. Press, then remove the tacking. Top stitching is an attractive alternative, or any of the other methods of edging given above. A card template cut in the same way as the seam guide helps to keep hems even in width.

Rouleau

This is a very useful technique to master, since from rouleau you can make ties, belts, bows and contrive innumerable trimmings. For instance, a simple idea would be to plait three rouleaux to make a tie belt. Rouleau can be made in two ways; try both methods and choose the one that suits you best.

First method Cut a strip of fabric the length required, following the grain of the material. Fold the strip in half lengthwise, right sides together. Join the edges using a 1 cm (⅜ in) flat seam (diagram 17).

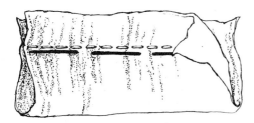

Diagram 17   *First method of making rouleau (first stage)*

Using a pen, the head of a knitting needle or some other thin, blunt-ended utensil, turn the cheesecloth through to the right side (diagram 18). This is not always as easy as it sounds, especially if the strip to be turned is long. You could try attaching a safety pin to the end of the strip and using this to turn the strip. To finish the rouleau, turn in the raw ends and oversew to neaten.

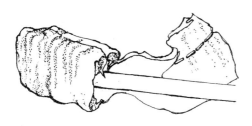

Diagram 18   *First method of making rouleau (second stage)*

Second method Make the cheesecloth strip into a band by turning 1 cm (⅜ in) to the wrong side along each long edge (diagram 19). Crease into place between thumb and forefinger and press, if necessary.

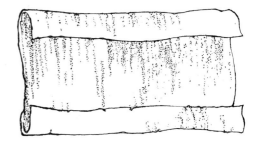

Diagram 19   *Second method of making rouleau (first stage)*

Fold the band in half so that all the raw edges are enclosed, and the wrong sides are facing. Oversew, or top stitch close to the edge (diagram 20). Finish off as for the first method.

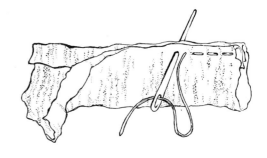

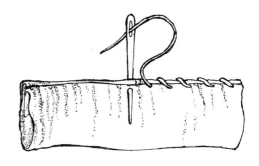

Diagram 20   *Second method of making rouleau (second stage)*

Top stitching

Top stitching is useful for securing hems; if you use a contrasting thread it can be very decorative too.

With the right side 'of the fabric towards you, turn the hems to the *front*, press and tack into place. If top stitching by hand, use a running or back stitch. Keep the stitching as straight as possible, and close to the edge of the fold. It is more important for the stitches to be even in length than to be small.

If you are using a sewing machine, first check the tension and adjust if necessary. (The manufacturer's instruction book will tell you how to do this.) Before you start, pull the top and bottom thread behind the presser foot so that they will not tangle in the sewing. Then stitch close to the edge of the hem, using the presser food or sewing guide to help you. You can buy extra thick machine thread that is intended for top stitching — it is very effective. If you have a zigzag sewing machine or a machine capable of embroidery you will find many other stitches which can be used for top stitching — the simplest of which is to set your machine to a medium length stitch and a medium swing.

Attaching lace

First method Use this method to attach lace which has a finished edge. Turn and stitch a narrow hem on the piece of cheesecloth to be edged. Place the right side of the lace to the right side of the cheesecloth, keeping the edges level. Pin and tack into place. Oversew the lace to the fold of the hem (diagram 22). Remove the tacking and press the lace downwards.

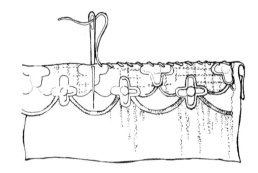

Diagram 22   *First method of attaching lace*

Second method Use this method to attach lace which has an unfinished edge, such as broderie anglaise. Place the wrong side of the lace to the wrong side of the cheesecloth. Arrange them so that you can stitch through both fabrics. Pin and tack into place. Work the first part of a french seam (diagram 23). Be particularly careful when trimming the edges.

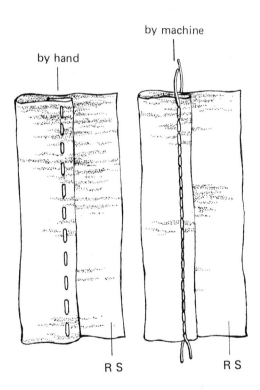

by machine

by hand

R S   R S

Diagram 21   *Top stitching*

Diagram 23   *Second method of attaching lace (first stage)*

Fold so that the right sides of the lace and cheesecloth are facing. Work the second part of the french seam (diagram 24). Remove the tacking and press the lace downwards.

If you are adding lace to an article and have to use this method, read through the instructions carefully, you might have to change the order of making up so that you can attach the lace to an unhemmed edge. It is also worth remembering that if you use broderie anglaise you will have to iron it after washing.

Diagram 24   *Second method of attaching lace (second stage)*

BEFORE YOU START

Pre-shrinking

Some cheesecloth fabrics, especially if they are very loosely woven, can shrink to quite a degree. If you are not certain whether the fabric you are buying will shrink or not, it is best to pre-shrink it. This means that you will have to buy approximately ten per cent more fabric than called for in the pattern. For example, instead of 1.40 m (1½ yd), you will need to buy 1.55 m (1⅝ yd). Wash the cheesecloth in hot water (60°C/140°F) for medium wash, or leave it to soak in very hot water until the water cools enough to wash the cheesecloth by hand. Spin or wring, allow to dry, then press.

If, after all, your cheesecloth has not shrunk, you will have extra material to make some of the smaller items in this book.

Measurements

Where there is a choice of sizes, check the measurements given and decide which size you intend to make. If you like your clothes to be close fitting it is worth considering making a smaller size. You might also want to adjust the length of a garment, and instructions for this are given for each item.

Since converting metric and imperial measurements accurately leads to fractions, (for instance 5 in is 12.5 cm and 60 cm is 23⅝ in) the measurements for each article or garment have been worked out separately. So if you cut out an article following the metric measurements, use metric for making up the garment as well.

Materials

Before the shops close, make sure that you have all the materials listed. It is particularly irritating to be unable to wear a garment because you have forgotten to get any elastic — or some such seemingly unimportant item. Make a list of all the items needed, and tick them off as you acquire them.

Cutting out

Carefully read through the cutting out instructions to make sure that you understand them. If you have any doubts, join sheets of clean newspaper together and have a trial run. Before you actually start cutting the cheesecloth, try and make sure you are not going to be disturbed for a while. Then, clear sufficient space and spread out the cheesecloth on a clean surface. Mark out the cheesecloth, cut out with the sharp dressmaking scissors and label the pieces as you cut.

Labelling

Labelling is useful if many pieces have to be cut for a particular garment, or if several bits of a garment are approximately the same size. Either write on the cheesecloth, using tailor's chalk, or write on slips of paper and pin these to the fabric. In either case use the name of the piece as given in the cutting out instructions. Make sure that you always label the right *or* the wrong side of the fabric, or you can easily get confused when making up.

Making up

Check through the instructions for making up. If you are not sure about any of the steps involved, pin or tack the garment together — it is so much easier than trying to visualize the result. If you find sewing tedious, or know that your enthusiasm quickly evaporates, a great morale booster is to make a list of the stages involved and cross them off as you complete them. It does make you feel that you are getting somewhere, even if the garment is still in pieces.

Storage

Some articles in this book will take more than one evening to complete and will need to be stored between sessions. Slip them inside a clean pillowcase or plastic bag, either of which can be pinned to a wire coat hanger and hung up out of the way. As a garment progresses it can be put onto the hanger and the bag or pillow case can be slid over the top. Try to avoid putting an unfinished article completely out of sight; all too often it never gets finished. Out of sight out of mind — until suddenly you want to wear it.

For safety's sake never leave plastic bags where children can play with them. They may not be able to read the warnings printed on them — but you can.

Left-handed sewing

The diagrams in this book are intended for right-handed people, and if you are left-handed you might have difficulty interpreting them. I suggest that you use a mirror and work from the reflection. Prop open the book and place a mirror against the opposite page. Adjust the book and mirror so that you can see the diagram's reflection. Work from this reflection, which, of course, will be the reverse of the diagram in the book.

CARING FOR CHEESECLOTH

Having devoted time and effort to making a garment it would be distressing to ruin it. The easiest way to prolong the life of clothes is to hang them up after each wearing.

Washing

Cheesecloth is a cotton fabric and washes well. It normally dries quickly too. It is best washed by hand in warm water and then left to drip-dry. It should not need ironing. If you are in a hurry, or have nowhere to drip-dry clothes, it can be put into a spin dryer for a short while — about fifteen seconds. It should then be shaken to get rid of as many creases as possible, and pulled into shape. You can machine-wash cheesecloth. Use warm water for the minimum time in a twin tub, or set an automatic for delicate fabrics. It is also fairly tolerant of being washed at the launderette, but does tend to need ironing after this treatment — or you can shake it vigorously and put it out on the washing line in a stiff breeze.

White cheesecloth Plain white cheesecloth can be washed in very hot water and bleached or boiled if necessary.

Home-dyed fabric Wash cheesecloth that has been dyed at home separately. It loses a little colour in the first few washes. Also, when drying such a garment turn it inside out, as home-dyed fabric can fade in bright sunlight.

Starching

Whilst it is a relief that nobody nowadays is obliged to wear collars starched so stiff that they leave red marks on the neck, I think that it is a pity that the other old-fashioned use of starch is overlooked. A diluted starch solution can restore and revive clothes, by replacing the original fabric dressing present when the garment was new. Buy some starch from your local store, and follow the instructions on the packet to make your clothes look like new again.

Ironing

For those who dislike unnecessary effort, and are always in a hurry, one of the joys of cheesecloth is that it does not need ironing. However, it can need touching up with the iron, and you may prefer to press the complete garment. If you do intend to iron cheesecloth, it is best done whilst it is slightly damp. Use a hot iron set for cotton. If the cheesecloth is dry you will have to damp it down. To do this flick water onto it, or cover it with a damp cloth. Try not to stretch the cheesecloth as you iron, as it is easily pulled out of shape. Also be careful that you do not catch embroidery with the point of the iron; cover the embroidery with a cloth before you start.

VERY SIMPLE SEWING

The garments that follow are all very simple to sew, intended for people who have never even considered making their own clothes before, or for people, like me, who want a dress that can be finished in an evening. They are all made from two rectangles of cheesecloth, so if you are already an expert dressmaker it will take you longer to get out and set up your sewing machine and heat up your iron than to actually stitch.

Sundress

This pretty dress will keep you cool on hot summer days, and the shoulder straps are adjustable for maximum comfort. It comes in three sizes to fit children and adults.

SUNDRESS

Large sundress
This will fit up to 95 cm (38 in) bust loosely, length 90 cm (36 in).

Materials
  2.2 m (2½ yd) cheesecloth
  thread to match
  2 m (2 yd) ribbon or cord to match or contrast

Cutting out   Fold the fabric in half and cut across the width to give two pieces each 110 x 90 cm (45 x 36 in) for back and front (diagram 25).

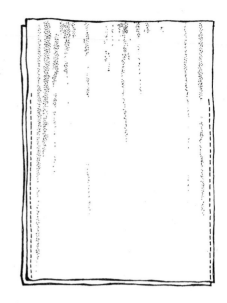

Diagram 26   *Joining the front and back*

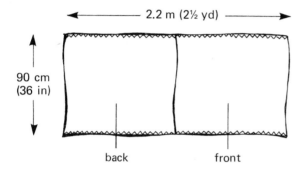

Diagram 25   *Cutting out the large sundress*

Making up   With right sides facing, pin and tack the longer edges of the back and front together. Work a 1.5 cm (⅝ in) flat seam along one edge, but leave 25 cm (10 in) unstitched to form the armhole. Sew a second seam in the same way, but make sure that both the openings are at the same end (diagram 26). Remove the tacking. Press the seams open along their entire length. They will not need neatening. The edges of the armhole should now be on the wrong side. Top stitch around the armhole.

Turn and stitch a 2.5 cm (1 in) hem between the armholes at the front and at the back (diagram 27). Remove the tacking and press. Turn and stitch a 10 cm (4 in) hem on the bottom edge. Cut the cord in half and thread one piece through the hem at the top of the back, and the second piece through the hem at the front. Knot the ends of the cord to stop it fraying, or if using ribbon cut the ends into a 'V'. Try on the completed dress and tie the cords at the shoulders.

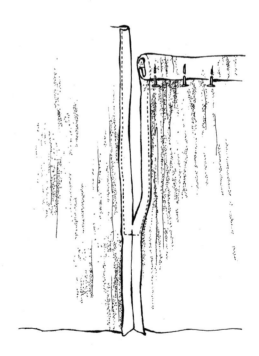

Diagram 27   *Top stitching the armhole and turning the top hem*

To adjust the length If only a small adjustment is necessary, simply make the bottom hem wider or narrower. To lengthen the garment considerably, work out how much longer you want your dress to be, double this measurement, and buy this much extra fabric. To shorten, work out the adjustment, double it, and take this away from the amount of fabric needed. Alternatively you could lengthen this garment by adding a frill (see the chapter on Frills and Flounces).

Medium sundress

This will fit up to 75 cm (30 in) chest loosely, length 75 cm (30 in).

Materials
    1.6 m (1¾ yd) cheesecloth
    thread to match
    2 m (2 yd) ribbon or cord to match or contrast

Cutting out Fold the fabric in half and cut across the width to give two pieces each 80 x 90 cm (31 x 36 in) for the back and front.

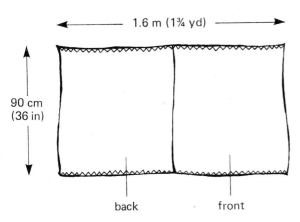

Diagram 28   *Cutting out the medium sundress*

Making up Make up as for the large dress, but leave only 30 cm (8 in) unstitched for the armholes. You will also have to neaten the edges of the seams and hem the armholes. You might find it useful to stitch through the centres of the bows once they are tied, so that a child can simply pull the dress on and off without having to retie them.

Small sundress

This will fit up to 50 cm (20 in) chest, length 35 cm (14 in). If you want to re-use some old fabric, you could make this toddler's dress from the best parts of an old cheesecloth shirt or skirt.

Materials
    45 cm (½ yd) cheesecloth
    thread to match
    1 m (1 yd) ribbon or cord to match or contrast

Cutting out Fold the fabric so that the selvedges match. Then cut between the selvedges to give two pieces each 45 cm (18 in) square, one for the back and one for the front (diagram 29).

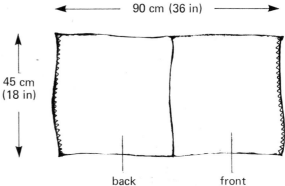

Diagram 29   *Cutting out the small sundress*

Making up With right sides facing, pin and tack the front and back together. Stitch the side seams, leaving 10 cm (4 in) unstitched to form the armholes. Neaten the seams, and top stitch the armholes. Turn and stitch a 2.5 cm (1 in) hem between the armholes at the front and back. Turn and stitch a 5 cm (2 in) hem on the bottom edge. Cut the cord in half and thread one piece through each top hem. Knot the ends of the cord to prevent them from fraying, or if using ribbon cut the ends into a 'V'. Try the completed dress on the child and tie the cords at the shoulders.

Evening Dress

This elegant full-length dress will suit any special occasion, and its lines are so classic that the style will not date. It will fit up to 95 cm (38 in) bust loosely, length 155 cm (60 in).

Materials
    3.3 m (3½ yd) cheesecloth
    thread to match
    1 m (1 yd) ribbon or cord to match or contrast

Cutting out   Fold the fabric in half and cut across the width to give two pieces each 170 x 45 cm (66 x 36 in) for the back and the front (diagram 30).

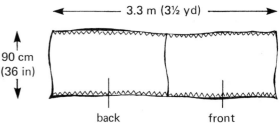

Diagram 30   *Cutting out the evening dress*

Making up   Make up as for the large sundress, but leave 27.5 cm (11 in) unstitched to form the armholes. Do not cut the ribbon but thread it through both of the top hems. Try on the dress and tie the ribbon at the neck. If you need to adjust length, adjust it in the same way as for the large sundress. For an extra special occasion pin an artificial flower over the bow (see page 58). You could adapt any of the sundresses to tie in this fashion, though you would have to make the armholes slightly bigger. You will only need one tie, but you could use the second tie as a belt.

EVENING DRESS

Gathered Skirt

This simple summer skirt with a tie waist can be worn as a slit skirt, or more formally as a wrap-over. You can make it long, midi length or short.

Long skirt
This will fit up to 70 cm (28 in) waist, length 100 cm (40 in.).

Materials
    2.5 m (2¾ yd) cheesecloth
    thread to match

Cutting out   Cut two 5 cm (2 in) strips across the width of the fabric for the ties. Fold the remaining fabric in half and cut across the width to give two pieces each 120 x 90 cm (48 x 36 in) for the main parts of the skirt (diagram 31).

To make up the main part, with right sides facing, pin and tack one selvedge of the front to one selvedge of the back. Work a 1.5 cm (⅝ in) flat seam along the entire length. Remove the tacking and press open. For the waist edge, turn and stitch a 2.5 cm (1 in) hem. Turn and stitch a 10 cm (4 in) hem at the bottom edge. Thread the tie through the top hem.

To adjust the length   If only a small adjustment is necessary, simply make the lower hem wider or narrower. To lengthen considerably, work out how much longer you want your skirt to be, double this measurement, and buy this much extra fabric. To shorten, work out the adjustment, double it and take this away from the amount of cheesecloth needed. When cutting out, make sure that you cut the ties first.

If you are going to wear this as a slit skirt consider making a matching garter (see page 92).

Diagram 31   *Cutting out the long gathered skirt*

Making up   With the right sides together, join the two short edges of the strip to make the tie. Use a 1.5 cm (⅝ in) flat seam. Press the seam open and make the tie into a rouleau. Neaten the ends.

GATHERED SKIRT

Midi skirt
This will fit up to 70 cm (28 in) waist, length 80 cm (32 in).

Materials
    2.1 m (2 ⅜ yd) cheesecloth
    thread to match

Cutting out   Cut two 5 cm (2 in) strips across the width of the fabric for the ties. Fold the remaining cheesecloth in half, and cut across the width to give two pieces each 100 x 90 cm (40 x 36 in), for the main parts of the skirt (diagram 32).

Making up   Make up as for the long skirt. Adjust the length in the same way too.

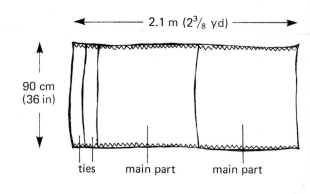

Diagram 32   *Cutting out the midi gathered skirt*

Short skirt
This will fit up to 70 cm (28 in) waist, length 65 cm (26 in).

Materials
    2 m (2 yd) cheesecloth
    thread to match

Cutting out   Cut a 5 cm (2 in) strip from one selvedge to make the tie. The remaining 200 x 85 cm (72 x 34 in) is the main part (diagram 33).

Making up   Make the strip into a rouleau, and neaten the ends. On the main part, turn and stitch narrow hems on both short sides. For the waist edge, turn and stitch a 2.5 cm (1 in) hem. Turn and stitch a 10 cm (4 in) hem at the bottom edge. Thread a tie through the top hem.

Adjusting the length   The length of this skirt can be adjusted only slightly, as it is dependent on the width of the fabric. However it is very effective if made with a fabric which has a border print.

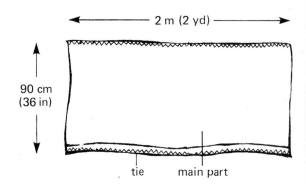

Diagram 33   *Cutting out the short gathered skirt*

Sun Top

This can be worn tied round the neck, or suspended from bows at the shoulders. It will fit up to bust 95 cm (38 in), length 45 cm (18 in).

Materials
    1.1 m (1¼ yd) cheesecloth
    thread to match

Cutting out   Cut two 5 cm (2 in) strips across the width of the fabric to make the ties. Cut the remaining fabric in half to give two pieces, each 45 x 90 cm (18 x 36 in) for the front and back (diagram 34).

1.1 m (1¼ yd)

90 cm
(36 in)

ties   back   front

Diagram 34   *Cutting out the sun top*

Making up   Make each strip into a rouleau and neaten the ends. You will need to make only one tie if you intend to wear the top tied close to the neck — but if you make up both ties you can vary the way you wear it to suit your mood. Make up the main part as for the large sundress, but turning a 5 cm (2 in) hem on the bottom edge.

To adjust the length   If only a small adjustment to the top is necessary, simply make the lower hem wider or narrower. To lengthen considerably, work out how much longer you want your top to be, double this measurement, and buy this much extra fabric. To shorten, work out the adjustment, double it and take this away from the amount of cheesecloth needed. You could of course adjust the length of this top by adding a frill (see the chapter on Frills and Flounces).

These extremely simple clothes could form the basis of a summer wardrobe. They look totally different made up in various forms of cheesecloth, for instance in checks and stripes. If you choose to make them up in plain cheesecloth, look through the rest of this book to discover the various ways in which you could decorate them.

SUN TOP

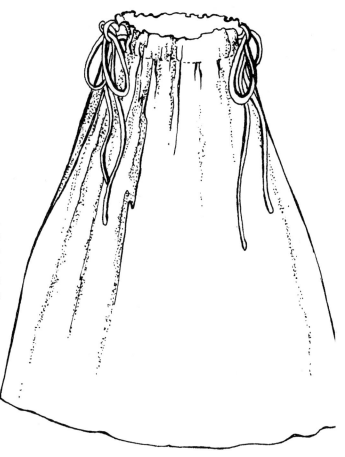

NEARLY AS SIMPLE

Instead of two rectangles, these shirts use four rectangles. If you follow the cutting out instructions carefully you will find them quite easy to make.

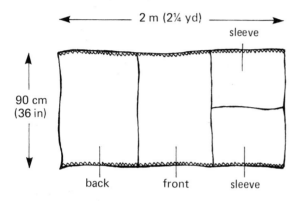

Diagram 35   *Cutting out the large basic shirt*

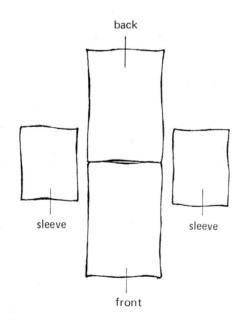

Diagram 36   *Arranging the pieces*

Basic Shirt

This loose fitting shirt can be made in three sizes. It has a boat neck and long sleeves. The side slits allow it be worn inside or outside jeans, belted or unbelted. If it is made in checked cheesecloth the checks will automatically match down the side seams. Alternatively you could make it in plain cheesecloth and give it a decorative edging.

Large shirt
This will fit up to 105 cm (42 in) chest or bust, length 75 cm (30 in), sleeve seam 40 cm (16 in).

Materials
2 m (2¼ yd) cheesecloth
thread to match

Cutting out   Across the width of the cheesecloth cut two pieces, each 70 x 90 cm (28 x 36 in). These are the back and front. Cut the remaining fabric in half between the selvedges to give two pieces each 60 x 45 cm (25 x 18 in) for the sleeves (diagram 35).

Making up   With the right sides together, join the shorter edges of the back and front (diagram 36). Use a flat seam, but leave 35 cm (14 in) unstitched at the centre for the neck opening (diagram 37). Press the seams open. You will not have to neaten them, but hem or top stitch the edges of the neck into place.

On the sleeves, mark the centre of the longer edge. Place them to the shoulder seams, with the wrong sides facing. Join using a french seam, and press.

Starting with the wrong sides together, join the sleeve and side seams in one continuous french seam (diagram 38). Leave 35 cm (14 in) unstitched at the bottom edge to form side slits. Neaten the edges. Turn and stitch 2.5 cm (1 in) hems on the sleeves. Turn and stitch 10 cm (4 in) hems on the front and back. Press.

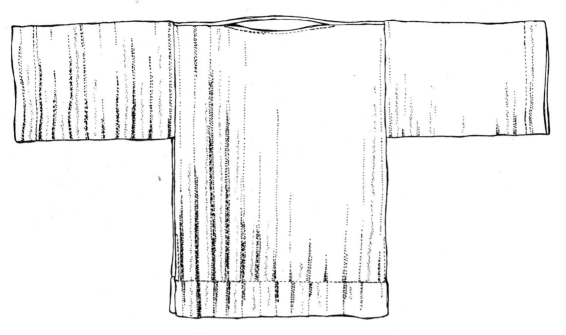

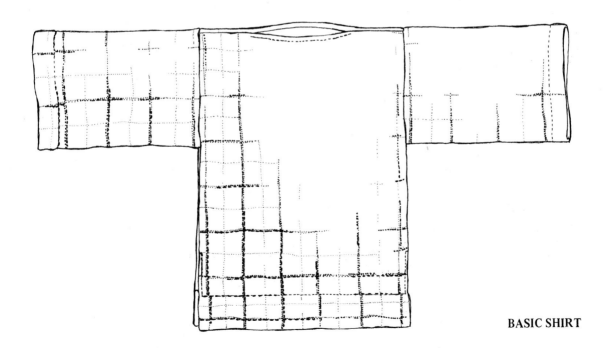

BASIC SHIRT

Diagram 37   *Making the neck opening*

Diagram 38   *Joining the sleeve and side seam to leave a slit*

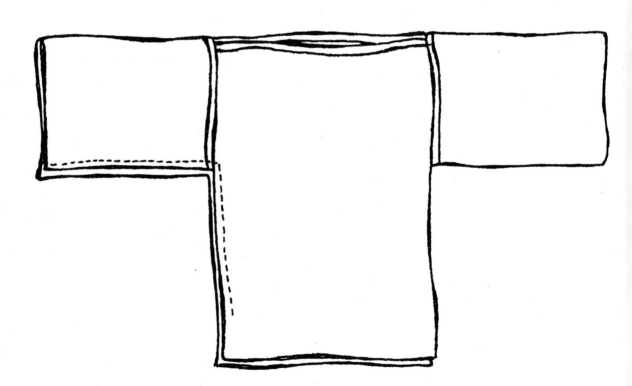

I prefer wide hems as they hold their shape, but you could cut 7.5 cm (3 in) from the front and back and then turn 2.5 cm (1 in) hems. You could use these oddments to make a matching tie belt.

To adjust the length If you want to make a longer shirt, turn only narrow hems on the back, front and sleeves. To make a shorter shirt, either make the hems wider, or cut a strip from the shorter edges of the front and back, and the longer edges of the sleeves. It would also be easy to make a short-sleeved version, by measuring how far down the arm you wanted the sleeve to come, and cutting the sleeve to that measurement plus hem and seam allowances.

Medium shirt

This will fit up to 90 cm (36 in) bust or chest, length 75 cm (30 in), sleeve seam 40 cm (16 in).

Materials
    1.8 m (2 yd) cheesecloth
    thread to match

Cutting out Cut the cheesecloth across the width to give three pieces, each 60 x 90 cm (24 x 36 in). Keep the two pieces for the back and front. Cut the remaining cheesecloth in half between the selvedges to give two pieces, each 60 x 45 cm (24 x 18 in) for the sleeves (diagram 39).

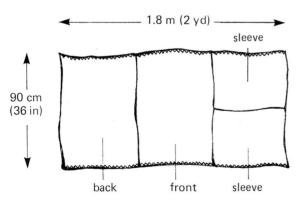

Diagram 39   *Cutting out the medium basic shirt*

Making up Make up as for the large shirt but make the neck opening 30 cm (12 in) long. Adjust the length if necessary in the same way, too.

Small shirt

This will fit up to 75 cm (30 in) chest, length 50 cm (20 in), sleeve seam 40 cm (16 in).

Materials
    1.1 m (1¼ yd) cheesecloth
    thread to match

Cutting out Cut the cheesecloth between the selvedges to give two pieces, each 110 x 45 cm (45 x 18 in). From each piece cut 50 x 45 cm (20 x 18 in) for the sleeve, leaving 60 x 45 cm (25 x 18 in) for the back and front (diagram 40).

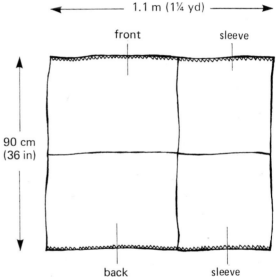

Diagram 40   *Cutting out the small basic shirt*

Making up Make up as for the large shirt, but make the neck opening 25 cm (10 in) wide, and the side slits 20 cm (8 in) long.

To adjust the length This shirt can be lengthened or shortened as for the large shirt, or it can be lengthened by buying extra cheesecloth. Work out how much longer you want the shirt to be: buy this amount of ·extra cheesecloth. Remember to add extra length to both the back and front when you cut them out. To shorten, buy less fabric.

Long Shirt

This is a simple adaptation of the basic shirt, so it can be made in the same three sizes, but will be approximately 5 cm (2 in) longer. Again, it looks attractive in checked cheesecloth, but for a special effect make it in a plain cloth and add embroidery to the front.

Cutting out   As for the basic shirt

Materials   As for the basic shirt.

Making up   Follow the instructions for making up the basic shirt, but do not turn up the bottom hem or neaten the side slits. Round off the bottom corners, using a plate or dish as a guide to draw round with tailor's chalk. Turn narrow hems on the bottom edges, rounded corners and side slits. You will have to make a row of running stitches at the corners. Gather these stitches up so that the hem lies as flat as possible. Pin into place carefully (diagram 41). Tack, then hem or top stitch into place.

To adjust the length   This shirt can be shortened by cutting the required amount from the bottom edges, but it cannot be lengthened.

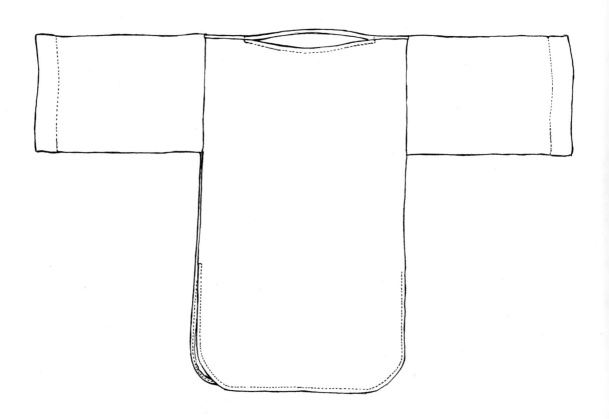

LONG SHIRT

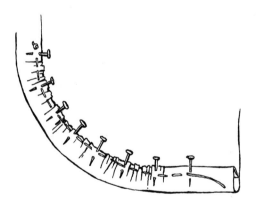

Diagram 41   *Hemming the bottom rounded corners*

Shirt Dress

This garment can be worn as a midi tunic dress, tied with a belt as a knee length dress, or worn in either fashion as an overshirt with trousers. It will fit up to bust 95 cm (38 in) very loosely, length 115 cm (46 in) when unbelted.

Materials
    3.6 m (4 yd) cheesecloth
    thread to match

Cutting out Cut the cheesecloth into two lengths across the width. Make the first length 240 x 90 cm (96 x 36 in) and the second length 120 x 90 cm (48 x 36 in) (diagram 42).

Cut a 10 cm (4 in) strip from the selvedge of the first length of cheesecloth. This is for the belt. Cut the remaining cheesecloth in half to give two pieces, each 80 x 120 cm (32 x 48 in) for the back and front. Round off the bottom corners of the back and front, using a plate or dish as a guide.

Cut a strip 30 cm (12 in) wide from the selvedge of the second length of cheesecloth (diagram 43). This is spare fabric. Cut the remaining piece in half to give two pieces, each 60 cm (24 in) square for the sleeves.

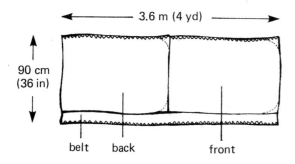

Diagram 42 *Cutting out the shirt dress (first length)*

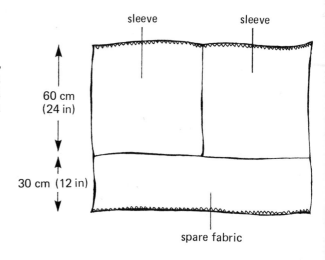

Diagram 43 *Cutting out the shirt dress (second length)*

Making up Make the strip for the belt into a rouleau, and neaten the ends. To complete the garment follow the instructions for making up the long shirt.

To adjust the length To lengthen, first work out how much longer you want your dress to be, double this measurement, and buy this much extra cheesecloth. To shorten, work out the adjustment, double it, and buy this much less cheesecloth.

Whether lengthening or shortening your dress, do remember to adjust the length of the back and front as you cut them — more especially remember to adjust the length of the first piece of cheesecloth that you cut.

Spare fabric The cheesecloth left over from this dress could be used to make pockets (see pages 70 and 76), or use the spare fabric to make some of the smaller items in this book.

SHIRT DRESS WITH BELT

DYEING CHEESECLOTH

Dyeing is by far the easiest way to completely change the look of a garment, and being a cotton fabric, cheesecloth is very easy to dye at home. But do not use dyeing to cover marks and stains; it tends rather to show them up. So before you start, make sure that the fabric is clean and that any spots have been removed.

The simplest, quickest and least messy way of dyeing at home is to use a brand of dye which can be applied in the washing machine, such as Wash'n Dye by Dylon (UK) or Rit (USA). Follow the instructions given by the manufacturer. With one tub of dye you should be able to dye two dresses or four tops, or three skirts, or a dress, top and skirt. In time the colour fades, but it is so easy just to add a further tub of dye to the washing machine and perk up the colour.

The only truly colour-fast dyes available for home use are cold water dyes. They are rather more complicated to use and you must follow the directions on the packet carefully. For each 250 grams (8 ounces) of fabric to be dyed you will need one tin or packet of dye, one tablespoon of washing soda (or a packet of cold dye fix) and four tablespoons of salt. The thing most people tend to overlook is thoroughly wetting the fabric. The cheesecloth needs to be soaked. If it is not saturated the finished results are bound to be streaky or patchy.

washing soda (or cold dye fix)
salt
bowl, bucket or other large container

Method Before starting make sure that your container is large enough to hold the article to be dyed and enough water to cover it. Put most of the fabric into the polythene bag, leaving just a border showing. Hold the bag tightly in place with an elastic band. Put on your rubber gloves, then prepare the dye according to the instructions on the packet. If the dye is in a tin can, use a beer can opener to open it easily, then rinse the empty tin can with a little boiling water to get out the last of the dye powder.

Wet the part of the fabric to be dyed, then put it into the dye bath for about an hour. Remove it from the dye bath, squeezing out as much excess dye as possible first. Remove the polythene bag and move it up so that another band of cheesecloth shows. Replace the elastic band, wet and replace the cloth in the dye bath for a further hour. After this, move the bag up to expose a third band of undyed fabric, and dye again. Finally, remove the cheesecloth from the dye bath, leaving the polythene bag in place. Rinse thoroughly in cold water, and continue rinsing until the water runs clear. Then remove the polythene bag, and give the complete article a final rinse. Allow to dry.

Dip Dyeing

This gives graduated bands of colour and is extremely effective. It takes time, but is a very straightforward process.

Equipment
    rubber gloves
    polythene or plastic bag (large enough to hold
      the article to be dyed)
    elastic bands
    cold water dye

Dip-Dyed Dress

This dress has a dip-dyed skirt joined to a separately dyed top. It is adapted from the frilled dress on page 91. You will need 6 m (7 yd) of plain cheesecloth. Cut out following the first part of the instructions, then make up the top and skirt but do not join them together yet. Put the top into the dye bath. Dip dye the skirt to give three bands of colour. Remove the skirt and top from the dye bath, rinse and dry them, then attach the skirt to the top following the instructions given on page 92.

DIP-DYED DRESS

Tie And Dye

The idea is to make patterns on the cheesecloth by tying it so that the dye cannot penetrate to certain parts of the fabric. (This is exactly what happens if you do not wet the fabric thoroughly before you dye — the difference being one of intent.)

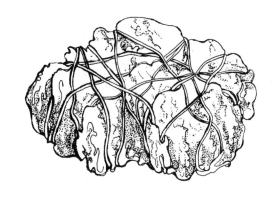

Equipment
    rubber gloves
    elastic bands or thick string
    cold water dye
    washing soda (or cold water fix)
    salt
    bowl, bucket or other large container

Diagram 44   *Tying for marbling*

Method   Before you start, check that your container is large enough to hold the cheesecloth to be dyed and enough water to cover. Then tie the fabric with the elastic bands or string and follow the directions for dyeing. There are many ways of tying the fabric, but the ones given below are the easiest and most effective.

Marbling   This is extremely easy to do, but for the very best results it needs to be dipped twice, preferably first in a light colour and then in a darker colour.
    Crunch the cheesecloth up in your hand, crush and squash it into as small a ball as you can. Slip elastic bands over the ball, and make them as tight as possible (diagram 44). Now dye the fabric.

Pleating   This will give a very pleasing border. Fold the cheesecloth back and forth to give concertina pleats. Put elastic bands around the pleats at intervals, and make them as tight as possible (diagram 45). Now dye the fabric.

Ruching   This gives an all over pattern. You will need thick string or cord rather than elastic bands. Roll the cheesecloth loosely around the string. Tie the ends of the string together. Pull them tight so that the fabric crunches up (diagram 46). Now dye the fabric.

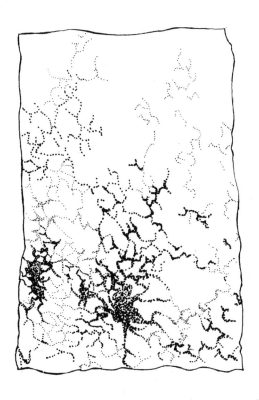

MARBLING (TIE AND DYE)

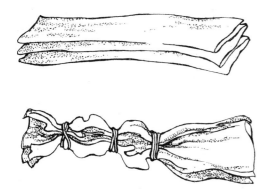

Diagram 45   *Tying for pleating*

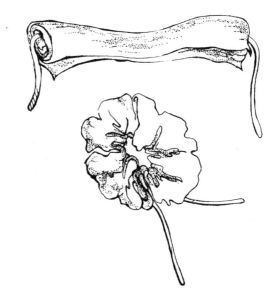

Diagram 46   *Tying for ruching*

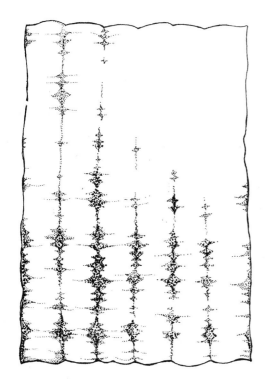

PLEATING (TIE AND DYE)   **RUCHING (TIE AND DYE)**

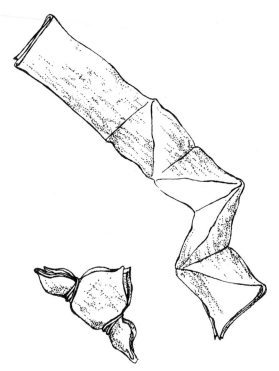

Diagram 47   *Tying for triangles*

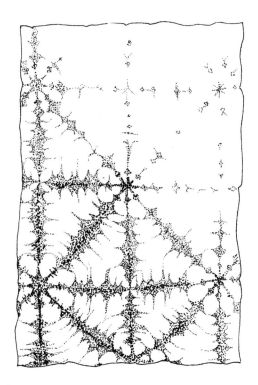

TRIANGLES (TIE AND DYE)

Triangles Fold the cheesecloth into four lengthwise, then, following diagram 47, fold it back on itself to form triangles. Put elastic bands tightly round two of the corners. Now dye the fabric.

Clump tying This produces undyed circles of cheesecloth and gives the greatest variety of patterns. You will need a great many small objects, such as buttons, marbles, plastic or metal bottle tops, or small stones.

Spread out the cheesecloth, and arrange the small objects on it in a pleasing pattern. Tie each object into the cheesecloth using an elastic band. Make sure that the elastic bands are as tight as possible. Now dye the fabric.

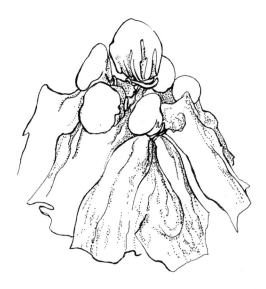

Diagram 48   *Clump tying*

Dyeing the fabric Make up a dye bath following the directions on the tin. Dip the tied cheesecloth quickly into water. This is the one occasion on which it should not be soaked before dyeing. Put the fabric into the dye bath and leave for about an hour. With rubber gloves on, take the fabric from the dye bath, having first squeezed out as much dye as possible. Rinse very thoroughly, make sure that the water runs clear. Cut through the rubber bands and remove them. Now (this is the really exciting bit) open out the fabric and allow to dry.

FRILLS AND FLOUNCES

Frills are so pretty, especially on children's clothes — but I find people are loath to try them. Perhaps they have been put off by fabric fraying, slipping or simply refusing to stay in place. This does not apply to cheesecloth; as it is a cotton fabric it is easy to work with. The second drawback, ironing and pressing, does not apply to cheesecloth either.

Attaching Frills

First method

Thread a needle with as long a length of thread as you can comfortably manage. Use the end of the thread which hangs from the reel — it will not tangle so easily. Fasten the thread onto the fabric firmly, close to the raw edge. Work of row of running stitch close to this edge. If you run out of thread, slip the needle off the thread and leave the end hanging. Fasten on a second length of thread. When you have completed the first row of running stitch, work a further row just below (diagram 49). Do not be tempted to miss out this second row, not only does it make the gathers more even, it can save time — should one thread break you are not going to have to start all over again. Alternatively you could use two rows of machine stitching; set your machine to its longest stitch.

Use the loose ends of thread to carefully pull up the gathers. If you have used machine stitching you will find it much easier to pull up the underneath thread (ie the one that comes from the bobbin). Place the right side of the frill to the right side of the main part. Adjust the gathers to fit, and hold in place with pins. Secure the gathers with more pins. Tack close to edge, then work the first part of a french seam. Be careful not to break the gathering threads when you remove the tacking (diagram 50). Fold the cheesecloth so that the wrong sides are facing. Pin and tack the gathers carefully, then work the second part of the french seam. Press the seam, but avoid flattening the frill.

If you want to attach lace to the frill, see page 17; do this before attaching the frill.

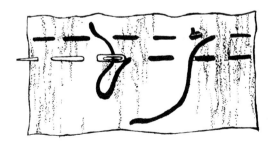

Diagram 49 *Gathering*

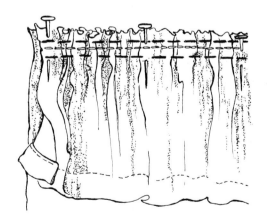

Diagram 50 *First method of attaching frills*

Second method

Turn and stitch a narrow hem on the edge of the frill to be gathered. Run a first gathering thread about 1 cm (⅜ in) from the hemmed edge of the frill. Run a second gathering thread just below this. Turn and stitch a narrow hem on the edge of the main part to which the frill is to be joined.

Place the main part right side up on a table or other flat surface. Place the frill on top, right side up, and overlap the edges by about 2.5 cm (1 in) (diagram 51).

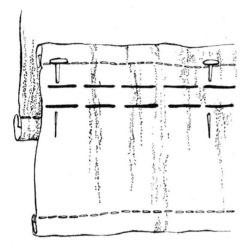

Diagram 51   *Second method of attaching frills (first stage)*

Pull up the gathering thread, and adjust the gathers to fit. Then pin and tack the frill into place. Top stitch the frill into place, by hand or machine, using matching or contrasting thread (diagram 52).

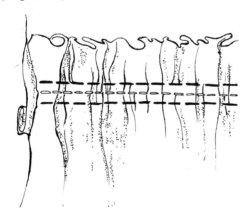

Diagram 52   *Second method of attaching frills (second stage)*

Shawl

At first glance this may seem an unusual shape for a shawl — but it can be worn in so many ways. As a shawl you can wear it with the point at the front or at the back and with the ends hanging loose. Wrapped round your shoulders, tied over one shoulder, or tied round your hips, it can team very fashionably with a frilled cheesecloth skirt. You can also wear it as a hood (with or without a hat) or as a top — with the ends crossed over at the front and tied at the back. Each side measures approximately 180 cm (72 in).

Materials
2.6 m (2⅞ yd) cheesecloth
threat to match
7.2 m (8 yd) lace edging (optional)
3.6 (4 yd) braid (optional)

Cutting out Across the width of the fabric cut eight 10 cm (4 in) strips for the frill. Cut the remaining cheesecloth in half between the selvedges to give two pieces, each 180 x 45 cm (72 x 18 in). Using diagram 53 as a guide, measure 45 cm (18 in) down one long edge. Cut from the opposite corner to this point. Cut a second piece in the same way — make sure that you have a matching pair. These are the main parts. The triangles you have cut off are spare fabric and could be used to make some of the smaller articles in this book.

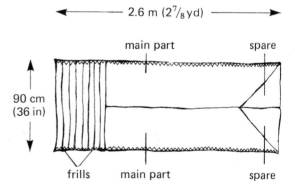

Diagram 53   *Cutting out the shawl*

Making up Join the slanted edges of the main parts together using a french seam. Remember to start with the wrong sides together. Pin and tack carefully; this seam is on the bias (ie across the grain of the fabric) and will tend to stretch. Press.

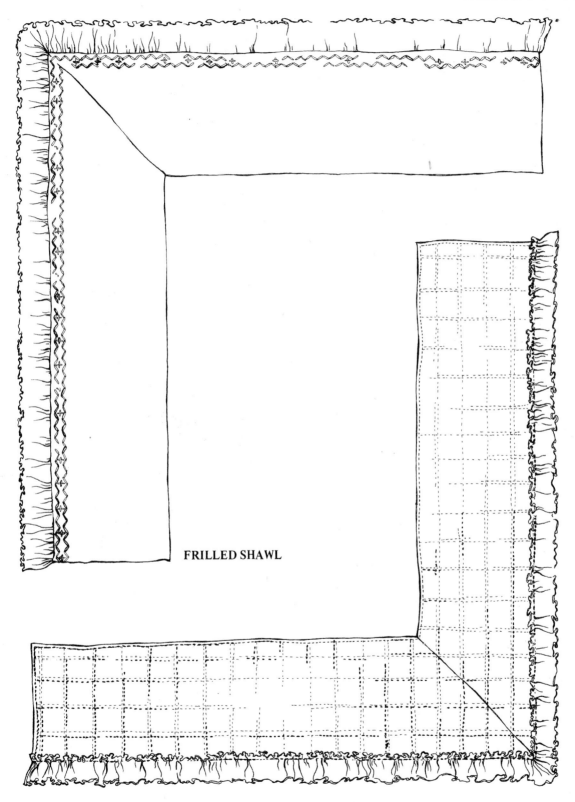

FRILLED SHAWL

Turn and stitch narrow hems on the inside of the 'V' and along the edges. Turn and stitch narrow hems on the short ends.

   With the right sides facing, join the short ends of the strips together to make one long frill. Use flat seams; you will not have to neaten the edges as they are all selvedges.

   Attach the frill (diagram 54) using the first or second method. Fold each long side of the main piece into four, and mark each point with a pin. Fold the frill into eight, and mark each point with a pin. Match up the pins. Pull up the gathering threads, and sew.

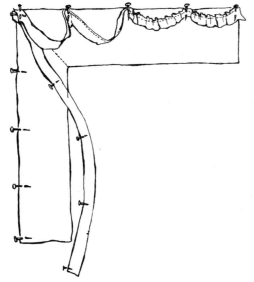

Diagram 54   *Attaching the frill*

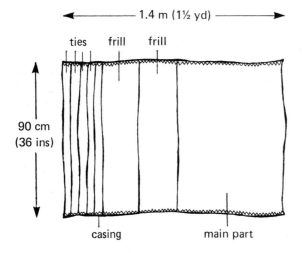

Diagram 55   *Cutting out the apron*

Apron

Pretty and practical, since it is so easily washed, this apron will brighten up your kitchen chores. Worn over a toning dress, it can also form a fashion outfit with a country-style flavour. These instructions are for an apron 90 cm (34 in) long.

Materials
   1.4 m (1½ yd) cheesecloth
   thread to match
   1.8 m (2 yd) lace edging (optional)

Cutting out   Cut five 5 cm (2 in) strips across the width of the cheesecloth for the ties and casing. Then cut two 20 cm (8 in) strips for the frill, leaving 75 x 90 cm (28 x 36 in) for the main part (diagram 55).

Making up   Join the short ends of two 5 cm (2 in) strips to make one long tie. Make it into a rouleau and neaten the ends. Do the same with a second pair of strips. Keep the remaining strip for the casing. Turn and stitch a 5 cm (2 in) hem on one short edge of the main part. Join the short ends of the frill using a flat seam, then press. Turn a narrow hem on the bottom edge, and attach the lace if you are using it. Attach the frill to the unhemmed edge of the main part.

   Thread one tie through the top hem, and try on the apron. Mark where you want the waist to be. Take the remaining strip for the casing. Fold 1.5 cm (⅝ in) to the wrong side on both long edges. With the wrong sides facing, place the folded casing over the marked waist, and pin into place (diagram 56). Use a tape measure to check that it is level. Pin, tack and then top stitch the casing into place.

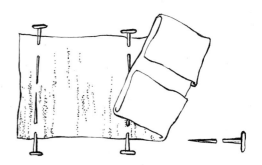

Diagram 56   *Making the casing*

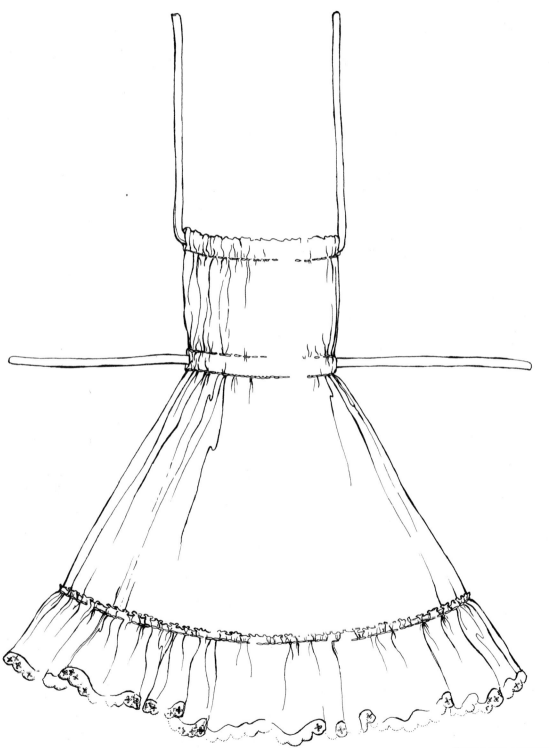

FRILLED APRON

Child's Apron

This is a good way of brightening up an old dress, or of disguising one that is too large. This apron measures 50 cm (20 in) in length.

Materials
   60 cm (¾ yd) cheesecloth
   3 m (3 yd) ribbon to match or contrast
   1.8 m (2¼ yd) lace edging
   thread to match

Cutting out From the selvedges of the cheesecloth, cut a 2.5 cm (1 in) strip for the casing, and three 20 cm (8 in) strips for the frill, leaving a piece 27 x 60 cm (11 x 27 in) for the main part (diagram 57). Cut the ribbon in half to give two ties.

Making up Neaten the ends of the ribbon ties. Turn and stitch narrow hems on both the short edges of the main part. Turn and stitch a hem wide enough to thread the ribbon through on one long edge. Using french seams, join the short ends of the frill pieces together to make one long frill. Turn and stitch narrow hems on the short ends and bottom hem. Then attach the lace. Attach the raw edge of the frill to the raw edge of the main part, using the first or second method. Finish off as for the large apron, but make the turnings on the casing narrower.

Adding Frills And Flounces

Any of the dresses and skirts in this book can have frills added. Work out how deep you want your frill to be, then add on 10 cm (4 in) for the seam and hem. Buy this much extra cheesecloth. When

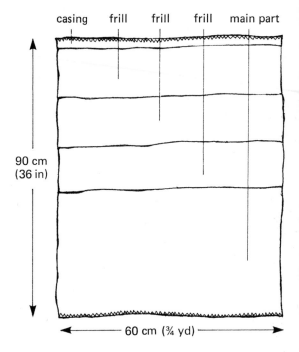

Diagram 57   *Cutting out the child's apron*

you are cutting out, always cut the ties first. Then cut three strips across the width of the fabric. Make each strip the width of the frill, plus 10 cm (4 in). Cut the remaining fabric in half across the width to give you the main parts of the garment.

Make up the garment following the instructions, but do not turn up the bottom hem. Join the short ends of the strips together to make one circular frill; make sure it does not get twisted in the middle, this is very easy to do. Attach the frill to the main part using the first or second method.

You can add a frill to make a garment longer. Decide how deep you want your frill to be, and add 10 cm (4 in). Buy three times this amount of extra cheesecloth, or this amount of another fabric if you want a contrasting frill. Cut out the main parts of the garment following the instructions, then cut the fabric for the frill into three strips, and make up the frill as explained above.

ELASTICATED SHIRRING

This technique is sometimes called ruching; it is easy to do and extremely effective. Since it involves many rows of stitching, you will need a sewing machine — it does not have to be capable of any fancy stitches, just straight stitching. Once you have mastered this technique you will find it easy to adapt patterns elsewhere in this book to give a ruched effect to bodices, waists and shoulders.

Ruching

Equipment
    shirring elastic
    thread to match or contrast
    sewing machine

Method Shirring elastic is normally sold in black and in white. For dark cheesecloth use black, and for light cheesecloth use white. Sometimes it is available in a wider range of colours; use a colour that matches rather than contrasts with your fabric. It comes wound on a spool, and has to be rewound onto the machine bobbin. This is best done by hand — try not to stretch it as you wind.

Put the bobbin containing the shirring elastic into your machine, and thread the top of the machine with ordinary cotton or synthetic thread. On the right side of the cheesecloth mark about 2.5 cm (1 in) from the edge. Use a row of tacking. With this side up, stitch along the line. Make sure that you leave at least 5 cm (2 in) behind the presser foot when you start.

Once you have finished the row gently ease the cheesecloth from underneath the presser foot and pull it back so that about 10 cm (4 in) of thread and elastic show. Cut the thread and elastic. Try not to tug sharply or you will find that, as you cut the elastic, it disappears back into the bobbin and has to be retrieved — and the other end withdraws through the stitching and cannot be retrieved. You have to stitch the whole row again.

Work further rows of stitching parallel to the first. It helps if you make yourself a card guide, or use a quilting foot if your machine has one.

Once you have finished the shirring, firmly tie off all the ends of elastic and thread. To tighten the shirring steam it. For a small article hold it over a steaming kettle or a pan of boiling water. For a larger article hold or hang it over the bath whilst you run hot water.

Shirred Dress

This figure-hugging dress is smart and practical — the shoulder ties can be fastened round the neck for a halter effect, or crossed at the back of the shoulders for an extra touch of interest. It will fit up to 95 cm (38 in) bust, length 100 cm (40 in).

Materials
    2.5 m (2¾ yd) cheesecloth
    thread to match
    shirring elastic
    thread to match or contrast for shirring

Cutting out Across the width of the fabric cut four 5 cm (2 in) strips for the straps. Cut the remaining cheesecloth in half to give two pieces, each 115 x 90 cm (45 x 36 in) for the back and front (diagram 58).

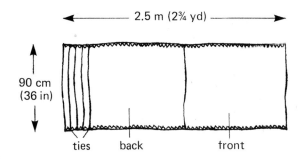

Diagram 58 *Cutting out the shirred dress*

SHIRRED DRESS

Making up Make the strips into rouleaux and neaten both ends of each. With the right sides facing, join one selvedge of the back to one selvedge of the front, using a flat seam. Press open. Turn a 2.5 cm (1 in) hem on one raw edge. This is the top. Work the first row of shirring close to the edge of the hem. Work a second row close to this to give extra strength. Work further rows about 1.5 cm (½ in) apart to a depth of 30 cm (12 in).

To complete the dress, join the remaining selvedges together, with rights sides facing. Use a flat seam, and make sure that all the ends of elastic and thread are enclosed in the seam. On the remaining raw edge (the bottom hem) turn and stitch a 10 cm (4 in) hem. Try on the dress and get someone to mark where the straps should go. Sew the straps firmly into place. Make sure the oversewing goes through the shirring, not just the edge of the hem, as the hem could tear under the strain.

To adjust the length To adjust the length slightly, make the lower hem wider or narrower. To lengthen it considerably, work out how much longer you want your dress to be, double this measurement, and buy this much extra cheesecloth. To shorten, work out the necessary adjustment, double it and take this amount from the cheesecloth needed.

This dress is very easy to adapt. If you worked only two or three rows of shirring you could wear it as a skirt or as a dress.

Child's Shirred Dress

This dress follows the style of the large shirred dress, and will fit up to chest 75 cm (30 in), length 75 cm (30 in).

Materials
    1.6 m (1 ¾ yd) cheesecloth
    thread to match
    shirring elastic
    thread to match or contrast for shirring

Cutting out Across the width of the fabric cut two 5 cm (2 in) strips. Cut each strip in half to give four straps, each 45 cm (18 in) long. The remaining piece, which should be 150 x 90 cm (59 x 36 in), is the main part (diagram 59).

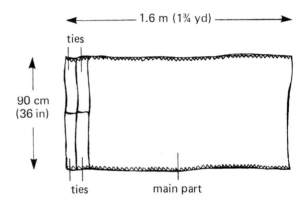

Diagram 59 *Cutting out the child's shirred dress*

Making up Make the strips into rouleaux and neaten both ends to complete the straps. On one selvedge turn and stitch a 2.5 cm (1 in) hem. This is the top edge. Work the first row of shirring close to this edge. Work a second row close to the first for extra strength. Work further rows about 1.5 cm (½ in) apart to a depth of 25 cm (10 in). Complete this dress as for the adult's dress above.

To adjust the length To adjust the length slightly, alter the width of the bottom hem. To shorten considerably, cut a strip from the bottom edge of the main part. You cannot make this dress much longer, unless you add a frill (see page 46).

Bloused Tunic Top And Belt

The belt, cunningly made from pinch pleat curtain tape, makes a stunningly eye-catching feature on this simple top. Its effect matches the shirring on the shoulders, but has not actually been made in the same way. This is because narrow bands of shirring tend to roll over on themselves, so a shirred belt would be rather uncomfortable to wear. This top will fit up to 95 cm (38 in) bust, length 80 cm (32 in).

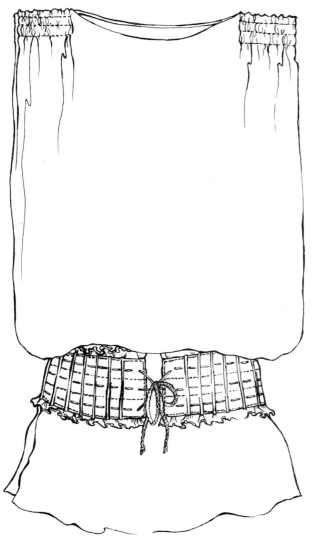

BLOUSED TUNIC TOP

Materials

    1.5 (1⅝ yd) cheesecloth
    thread to match
    shirring elastic
    thread to match or contrast for shirring and top stitching belt
    1.8 m (2 yd) of pinch pleat curtain tape 7.5 cm (3 in) wide

Cutting out Across the width of the cheesecloth cut two strips, each 15 cm (5 in) wide for the belt. Cut the remaining fabric in half across the width to give two pieces, each 60 x 90 cm (24 x 36 in) for the back and front (diagram 60).

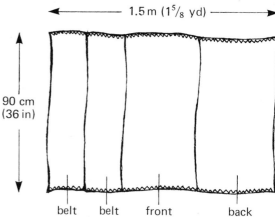

Diagram 60   *Cutting out the bloused tunic*

Making up With right sides facing, and using a flat seam, join the selvedges of the front and back, but leave 30 cm (12 in) unstitched at the centre to form the neck opening (diagram 61). Press the seam open along its entire length. Hem or top stitch the neck edges into place.

Turn and tack 1.5 cm (⅝ in) hems at the shoulder edges. Measure and mark with tacking 15 cm (6 in) from the shoulder edge (diagram 62). Work three rows of shirring about 1.5 cm (½ in) apart, on either side of the seam (diagram 63). Work the second shoulder to match.

With the right sides facing, join the side seams, but leave 30 cm (12 in) unstitched at the top for

Diagram 61   *Making the neck opening*

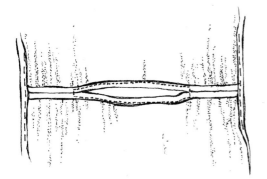

Diagram 62 *Neatening the neck and shoulder hems*

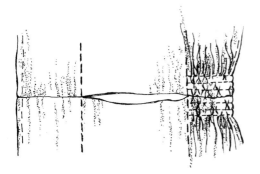

Diagram 63 *Shirring the shoulders*

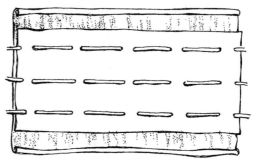

Diagram 64 *Laying the belt tape on the cheesecloth*

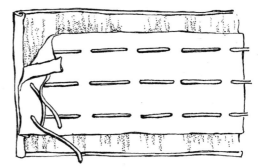

Diagram 65 *Neatening the ends of the belt*

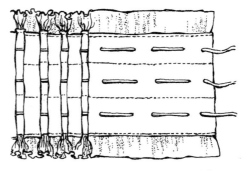

Diagram 66 *Top stitching and gathering the belt*

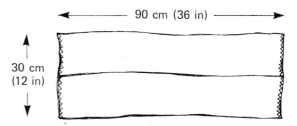

Diagram 67 *Cutting the belt from an oddment*

the armholes. Use a 1.5 cm (⅝ in) flat seam. Press the seam open along its entire length. Finish folding the hems to neaten the armholes, then hem or top stitch into place. Neaten the seams. Fold and stitch a 5 cm (2 in) hem on the bottom edge.

Making up the belt With the right sides facing, use a flat seam to join the short edges of the strips together. Press the seam open. Turn and stitch narrow hems on both of the long edges. The short edges and selvedges will not need neatening.

Place the cheesecloth wrong side up on the table, then put the curtain tape on top, wrong side down. Make sure that some fabric shows from underneath each side of the tape, then tack them together (diagram 64).

Neaten the ends of the belt. Make sure that you do not stitch through the cords of the curtain tape, or you will not be able to draw up the belt (diagram 65).

Work four rows of top stitching as shown in diagram 66. Remove all the tacking. Pull up the cords of the curtain tape until the belt fits loosely round your hips. Plait the cords together on each side, and finish each plait with a knot. Tie the plaits to fasten the belt.

This belt can be made and worn without the tunic, using an oddment of cheesecloth cut in half (diagram 67) to give two pieces each 15 x 90 cm (6 x 36 in). If you prefer, leave the cord ends unplaited, and you have a belt that you can adjust to fit your waist or your hips, depending on your mood. This would be particularly attractive if you knotted wooden beads to the ends of the cord.

Bloused Dress

The soft contours of this dress are harmoniously complemented by the shirring at the shoulders, the diamond-shaped sleeves and embroidery at centre front. It will fit up to 95 cm (38 in) bust, loosely, length 110 cm (44 in) – but it will be shorter when the belt is added.

Materials

> 2.7 m (3 yd) cheesecloth
> thread to match
> shirring elastic
> thread to match or contrast for shirring

Cutting out Across the width of the cheesecloth cut two 10 cm (4 in) strips for the belt. Cut the remaining fabric in half to give two pieces, each 125 x 90 cm (50 x 36 in) for the back and front (diagram 68).

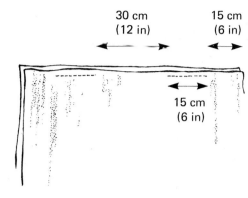

Diagram 69 *Making the neck and sleeve opening*

Now complete the dress following the instructions given above for the bloused tunic top, but leave the sleeve unshirred (diagram 70). Turn a 10 cm (4 in) hem at the bottom edge.

If adding embroidery, see pages 81-89, and complete the embroidery before making up.

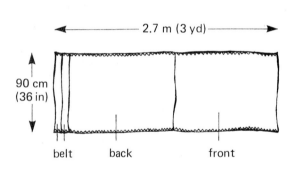

Diagram 68 *Cutting out the bloused dress*

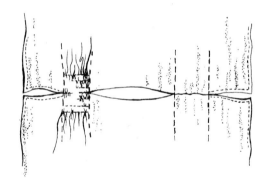

Diagram 70 *Shirring the shoulder*

Making up Join the short edges of the belt using a flat seam, then press. Make it into a rouleau, then neaten the ends.

With right sides facing, join the short shoulder edges of the front and back. Use a flat seam, but leave 30 cm (12 in) unstitched at the centre for the neck opening, and 15 cm (6 in) unstitched at each end to form the slit sleeves (diagram 69).

To adjust the length To adjust the length of this dress slightly, make the lower hem wider or narrower. To lengthen considerably, work out how much longer you want the dress to be, double this measurement, and buy this much extra fabric. To shorten, work out the adjustment, double it, and buy this much less cheesecloth. In either case make sure that you add or take away this amount from the length of the back and front as you cut them out.

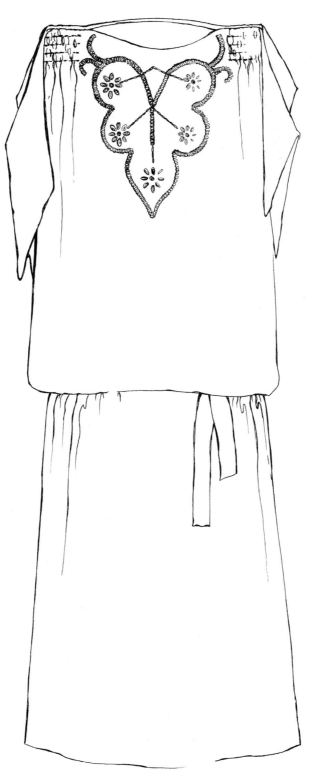

BLOUSED DRESS

Long Skirt

This skirt has a deep contrast frill and an elasticated waist, so with straps it can double as a dress. It will fit up to 100 cm (40 in) hips, length 100 cm (40 in). When teamed with a bandeau top, particularly if the bandeau matches the bottom frill, it makes a versatile outfit for holiday wear.

Materials
    1.4 m (1½ yd) cheesecloth for main part
    1.4 m (1½ yd) cheesecloth for frill
    thread to match
    shirring elastic
    thread to match or contrast for shirring

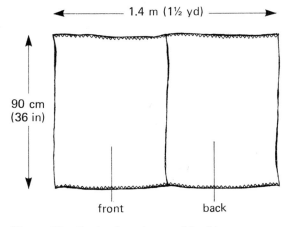

Diagram 71   *Cutting the main part of the skirt*

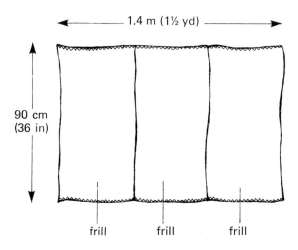

Diagram 72   *Cutting the strips for the frill*

Cutting out   Fold the fabric for the main part in half and cut across the width to give two pieces, each 70 x 90 cm (27 x 36 in) for the back and front (diagram 71). From the fabric for the frill cut three 45 x 90 cm (18 x 36 in) strips (diagram 72).

Making up   With the right sides facing, pin and tack the shorter edges of the back and front together. Work 1.5 cm (⅝ in) flat seams. They will not need neatening as they are selvedge edges. Press open. Turn and stitch a 5 cm (2 in) hem on one raw edge. Work three rows of shirring 1.5 cm (½ in) from the folded edge and 1.5 cm (½ in) apart. Using 1.5 cm (⅝ in) flat seams, join the short edges of the frill together to make one continuous length. Check that it is not twisted, and join the remaining short edges. Turn and stitch a 5 cm (2 in) hem on one edge. This is the bottom hem. Gather and attach the frill to the raw edge of the main part, following the instructions on page 41.

To adjust the length   To lengthen or shorten the skirt slightly, adjust the width of the bottom hem. Shortening or lengthening considerably can be done in two ways: either deepening or reducing the frill, or shortening or lengthening the main part. To change the depth of the frill, work out the adjustment and buy three times this amount less or extra cheesecloth. Similarly to change the length of the skirt, work out the adjustment, but this time buy double this amount less or extra cheesecloth.

Plain Skirt

This skirt is a slight variation of the one above, and can also be teamed with the bandeau top. It will fit up to 100 cm (40 in) hip, length 100 cm (40 in).

Materials
    2.8 m (3 yd) cheesecloth
    thread to match
    shirring elastic
    thread to match or contrast for shirring

Cutting out   Cut the cheesecloth in half across the width to give two pieces, each 140 x 90 cm (54 x 36 in), one for the main part, one for the frills.

Making up   Follow the instructions given above for the long skirt.

LONG SKIRT AND BANDEAU TOP

Bandeau Top

This attractive summer top can be made to match
any of the skirts in this book, or it can be teamed
with trousers or shorts as a sun top. It will fit up to
95 cm (38 in) bust, depth 20 cm (7 in).

Materials
    60 cm (⅝ yd) cheesecloth
    thread to match
    shirring elastic
    thread to match or contrast for shirring

Cutting out   Across the width of the fabric cut two
strips, each 5 cm (2 in) for the ties. Cut the remaining cheesecloth in half across the width to give two
pieces, each 20 x 90 cm (9 x 36 in) for the back and
front (diagram 73).

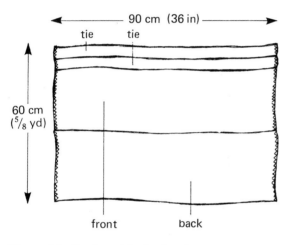

Diagram 73   *Cutting out the bandeau top*

Making up   With the right sides facing, pin and
tack the shorter edges of the back and front. Work
1.5 cm (⅝ in) flat seams. They will not need neatening as they are selvedges. Press open. Turn and
stitch 2.5 cm (1 in) hems on both raw edges. Work
two rows of shirring 1 cm (⅜ in) from the folded
edge and 1 cm (⅜ in) apart. Join the short ends of
the strips to make one long tie. Use a 1.5 cm (⅝ in)
flat seam, with right sides facing. Make this into a
rouleau, and neaten the ends.

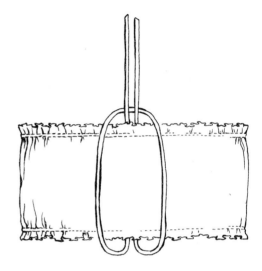

Diagram 74   *Tying the knot*

Loop the tie round the centre of the main part
as shown (diagram 74). Draw up the knot and tie
the ends behind your neck.

MOUNTED CUT OUTS

This technique is very easy, and is also very quick to do. It has many possible applications and extensions for costume jewellery and decoration.

Making The Cut Out

Equipment
- oddments of cheesecloth
- oddments of lightweight iron-on interlining
- an iron
- a sheet of clean paper
- sharp scissors
- small transfer design

Method
Collect several colours and textures of cheesecloth; you could dye some oddments if necessary. If you do not already have oddments of interlining, you can buy it in small packets, intended for stiffening collars and cuffs. Select pieces of cheesecloth and pieces of interlining of approximately the same size. Turn the iron to its hottest setting, and allow it to heat up.

Put a sheet of clean paper on the ironing board; this stops any glue from the interlining getting onto the ironing board cover — and once on it is extraordinarily difficult to get off. Place the cheesecloth on the paper, wrong side up. Put the interlining on top, adhesive side down (this is the shiny, rather rough side). Bond the fabrics together with the hot iron. Be careful not to let the edges of the interlining curl up; if it does, the glue will adhere to the iron and will be difficult to remove. Take bonded cheesecloth off the paper; you might have to peel it off if the loose edges of the interlining have become stuck.

Transfer your design to the interfacing. Cut out the shape very carefully, using the sharpest scissors you have.

Passementerie

If you wish you can couch braid around the edge of the cut out shape, and add sparkle with sequins and beads. Passementerie used to be done with gold and silver or lace braid and semi-precious beads (mainly jet), but coloured braid and glass beads are excellent substitutes for making 'poor man's' passementerie.

Equipment
- oddments of braid
- sequins
- beads
- thread to match
- fabric adhesive

Method
Mount the cheesecloth and cut out the shape as described above. Choose a braid that bends easily: Russion or soutache braids are ideal (and you can get them in gold and silver). Alternatively use thick knitting wool or thin piping cord.

Place the braid at the edge of the shape, holding it in place with your thumb and forefinger. Couch it into place. To do this, make neat overcasting stitches, close together, so that the braid is held securely to the fabric along its entire length (diagram 75).

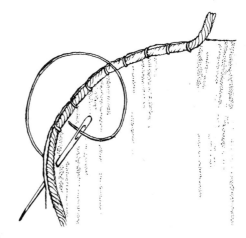

Diagram 75   *Couching*

Leave 1.5 cm (½ in) of cord loose at the beginning and the end. Take these ends to the wrong side of the shape and glue them carefully into place (see pages 10 and 62).

Use beads to attach the sequins, and make sure that they are firmly secured. Use more stitches than

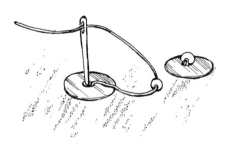

Diagram 76   *Attaching sequins*

you usually consider necessary to fasten on and off. It is worth the trouble in the long run — poorly attached sequins quickly work their way loose, and the whole article looks shoddy when this happens.

Diagram 77   *Pattern for flowers*

Choker

This eye-catching choker will complement any of the dresses or tops in this book. Quick to make, it costs almost nothing, and can be teamed with a matching bracelet or brooch.

Materials
    oddments of cheesecloth
    oddments of iron-on interlining
    tracing paper for patterns
    approximately 60 cm (24 in) narrow ribbon
    beads or buttons for flower centres
    thread to match

Cutting out Mount the cheesecloth onto the interlining as described above. Trace the flower shapes from diagram 77, and cut them out. Remember to use your paper-cutting scissors, not your dressmaking scissors. Using the shapes as patterns, draw round them on the interfacing and cut out several flower shapes from the bonded cheesecloth.

Making up Arrange the flower shapes in the centre of the ribbon. It looks better if the larger flowers are at the centre. Put several sizes together to make large, layered flowers. When you are satisfied with the arrangement, stitch the flowers firmly to the ribbon. Finally, sew a button or bead to the centre of each flower.

The choker can be tied round the neck, or, if you prefer, you can cut the ribbon to the exact measurement of your neck and sew on two hooks and eyes as fasteners. Add a small allowance to the neck measurement and sew under a small turning at each end to make a strong base for attaching the hooks and eyes.

Bracelet

To make a matching bracelet use a shorter length of ribbon and fewer, smaller flowers. For an alternative flower motif, see page 90. Again, the ribbon can be tied round the wrist to secure it, or it can be measured and cut to the exact size of the wrist (plus the turning allowance) and fastened with small hooks and eyes.

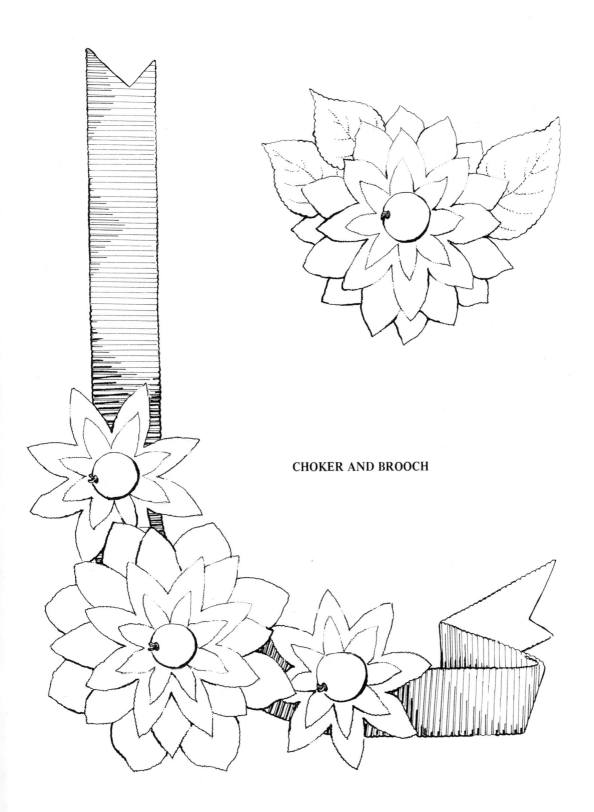

CHOKER AND BROOCH

Brooch

An attractive way to brighten up a plain dress, or turn a sundress into an evening dress is to add a flower brooch, on its own or teamed with matching jewellery.

Materials
> oddments of cheesecloth
> oddments of iron-on interlining
> tracing paper for patterns
> large bead or fancy button
> thread to match
> two or three metallic paper leaves (sold as cake decorations)
> small safety pin, or a cardboard badge (conference badge) and fabric adhesive

Making up   Cut out and make up one large flower, following the instructions given for the choker. Arrange the leaves at the back of the flower. Twist the wires of the leaves into loops and oversew them firmly to the back of the flower (diagram 78). If you are using a cardboard badge, glue it to the back of the flower so that the wire loops are covered up and there is no danger of them catching in clothes, or scratching skin. If you are using a safety pin, glue or oversew a small circle of cheesecloth over the wires. Finally, oversew the safety pin firmly into place. You could, of course, omit the pin and sew the flower directly to the garment.

You could add metallic paper leaves to a choker or bracelet, but you would have to use a second piece of ribbon to cover over the ends of the wire, or they would be extremely uncomfortable to wear.

Earrings

Earrings can be made by the same method as above. Make up small flowers, and neaten the backs. Glue the finished flowers to an old pair of earrings — or buy jewellery findings from a department store, which are very cheap. You could also make small holes in the flower petals and suspend them from hooped earrings.

Button-On Flowers

A fun idea is to put buttonholes in the centre of the flowers, made up as described above. The holes will not fray, as the interlining holds the fabric firmly. Fasten the flowers to the buttons of a ready-made shirt or dress, or sew buttons to one of the garments in this book, and make several sets of mix and match flowers.

Novelty Pendants

These appealing pendants can be hung from a chain necklace, or narrow ribbon. I have given three shapes and ideas for decorating them, but you could treat any simple shape in the same way. Look through children's picture books for inspiration. These examples use sequins for decoration, but a colourful alternative would be to use fabric paints, such as Dylon Fun Paints (UK), Fabri-Crylic Colors

Diagram 78   *Attaching the leaves*

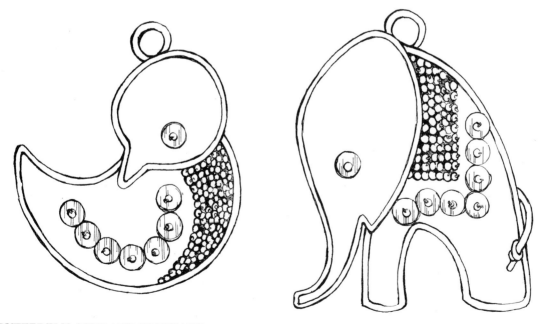

**BUTTERFLY, BIRD AND ELEPHANT
PENDANTS**

or Glad Rags Markers (USA). Follow the instructions given by the manufacturers. To turn the pendants into brooches, simply add a safety pin to the back.

Cutting out　Mount the cheesecloth on the interlining. Trace the chosen motif from the illustration. Cut it out and use it as a pattern for cutting the cheesecloth shape.

Materials
　oddments of cheesecloth
　oddments of iron-on interlining
　tracing paper for patterns
　oddments of braid or piping cord
　beads and sequins for decorations
　thread to match
　small curtain ring
　1 m (1 yd) narrow ribbon or chain necklace
　fabric adhesive

Making up the butterfly　Start couching the braid at the top of the butterfly's body (diagram 79). Finish at the same point, and glue the ends to the wrong side. Arrange the sequins and beads on the wings as shown in the illustration. Move them around until you find a pleasing pattern. Mark the centres of the sequins using a sharp pencil.

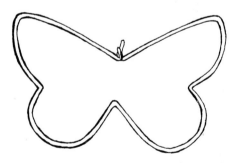

Diagram 79　*Couching the butterfly*

Stitch the sequins into place using beads. Oversew the curtain ring to the top of the shape. Thread ribbon through the ring and tie the ends into a bow, or use a chain necklace.

Making up the bird　Couch the braid round the main part of the body first, then glue the ends to the back (diagram 80).

Couch the braid round the head and beak, starting at the top of the beak, then glue the ends to the back (diagram 81). Position the sequin for the eye and sew it into place using a bead. If you wish, arrange extra sequins to mark the wing and breast.

Finish as for the butterfly, but you will find that the curtain ring has to be positioned off centre if the bird is to hang straight.

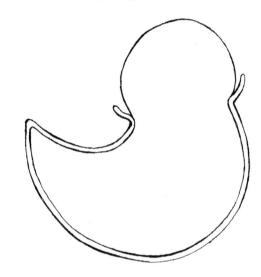

Diagram 80　*Couching the bird's body*

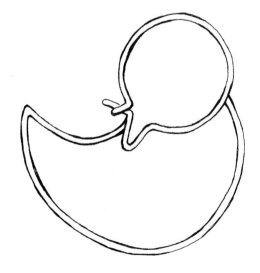

Diagram 81　*Couching the bird's head*

Making up the elephant Couch the braid round the main part of the body first, then glue the ends to the back (diagram 82).

Couch the braid round the head and trunk, starting at the chin, and glue the ends to the back (diagram 84).

Position the sequin for the eye and stitch it into place using a bead. Take a short length of braid for the tail. Tie a knot close to one end. Stick the unknotted end to the back of the elephant.

If you wish you can add extra beads and sequins to make a saddle cloth, or to decorate his feet and head. Complete the elephant as for the butterfly.

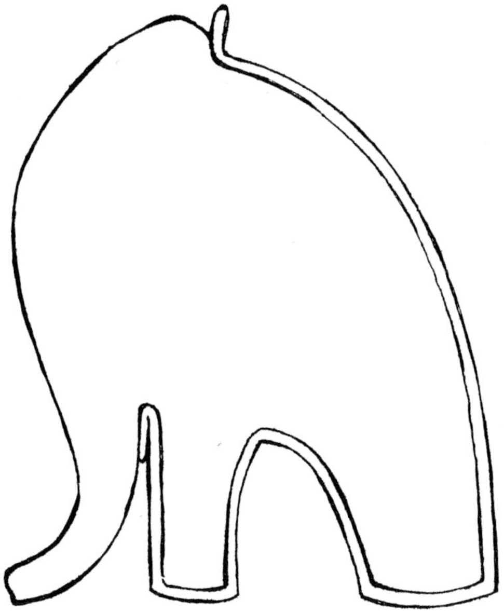

Diagram 82   *Couching the elephant's body*

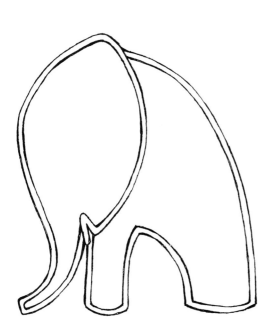

Diagram 83   *Couching the elephant's head*

Further Ideas

Mounted cut outs, with or without further decoration, have many applications. Cut out flowers or butterflies can be sewn to coloured combs to make pretty hair ornaments, and smaller versions of the cut outs attached to hairgrips will delight little girls. Try making a choker by attaching cut out butterflies wingtip to wingtip, and match this with a small butterfly nestling on a flower brooch.

The animal shapes make charming motifs for decorating (or patching) children's clothes, for example the baby's sundress on page 23, and extra flowers could also be used to decorate the front of the toddler's dress on page 93. Use a thick woollen yarn for couching the cut outs, and substitute brightly coloured paints for sequins and beads.

Cut out flowers and motifs can be used with equal success on adults' clothing: for example, the butterfly is used as a striking feature on the cowl neck top illustrated on page 67, and the smaller version of the butterfly could be substituted for the flowers used on the wedding dress on page 91. Also consider using cut outs instead of embroidery to decorate the lapels of the long jacket on page 84.

A pretty idea for the bloused dress on page 52 would be to cut out three butterflies or birds in descending size, and sprinkle them across one shoulder, or have them drifting across the scarves on pages 86, 88 and 89. The balanced repetition of a motif used in this way can add a sparkle of interest to a simply made garment. Flowers or cut out motifs could also be used to decorate the patch pockets of the hooded jacket on page 68, or the drawstring top on page 76. Look for suitable designs for your own cut outs, then look through this book for further applications.

DECORATIVE EDGINGS

Edging Techniques

Top stitching
This involves turning the hem to the right side of the fabric, and hand sewing in running or back stitch, or machine stitching, in a matching or contrasting coloured thread. See page 17 for full instructions.

Machine satin stitch
This is easy and effective, but requires a zigzag sewing machine. You can use ordinary sewing thread or machine embroidery thread, but beware, it takes a surprising amount of thread.

Thread the machine and adjust the stitch length to its minimum. The stitches should be almost on top of each other. Set the width of swing to its maximum. On a spare piece of cheesecloth, check the tension and adjust it as necessary. You should produce a band of satin stitch (diagram 84). If it is too open, adjust the length of the stitch. Stitch along the folded edge of the hem. You will find that the cheesecloth moves through the machine very slowly, and it is therefore easy to keep the stitching straight. Do not be tempted to pull the cheesecloth to speed up the process. If, after adjusting your machine, the stitching still looks ragged, work a second row on top.

Machine embroidery stitch
If you are lucky enough to have a machine capable of more complicated embroidery — experiment with it. Many of the stitches it produces can be used to secure hems.

Shell edging
This produces the prettiest, most delicate results, and after a little practice is easy to do. Use sewing thread to match or contrast with the fabric. Try and make the scallops as equal in size as possible (diagram 85). Draw up each scallop as you sew, and secure the hem with an additional back stitch.

Diagram 85   *Shell edging*

Machine scallops
This requires a zigzag sewing machine. Set the machine for its longest stitch and widest swing. Stitch carefully down the folded edge of the hem. Make sure that the left-hand stitches secure the hem, and that those on the right do not go through the material. This takes a little practice. Gently pull up the bobbin thread so that the scallops are formed. Knot the ends securely. The drawback of this method is that, if in wear the thread snaps, the whole hem rapidly comes undone.

Diagram 84   *Machine satin stitch*

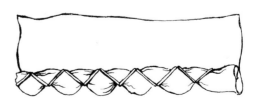

Diagram 86   *Machine scallops*

Cowl Neck Top

This go-anywhere top has full sleeves with elasticated cuffs. The cowl collar drapes beautifully in such a soft fabric as cheesecloth. It seems at first to require a rather extravagant amount of material, but the result is certainly worth it, especially since the spare pieces of fabric can be used to make patch pockets, or a pouch pocket (see page 76), or to make cut outs that can be sewn onto the garment (see page 57). This top will fit up to 95 cm (38 in) bust, length 60 cm (24 in), sleeve seam 60 cm (24 in).

Materials
  3.3 m (3¾ yd) cheesecloth
  thread to match
  thread to match or contrast for edging
  1.8 m (2 yd) narrow elastic
  paper for pattern

Cutting out   First of all cut a 90 cm (36 in) square from the fabric. Put this to one side for the cowl collar.

From the selvedge of the remaining fabric, cut a 25 cm (10 in) strip. This is spare. Then cut four pieces, each 60 x 65 cm (24 x 26 in); two are for the sleeves, and two for the back and front (diagram 87).

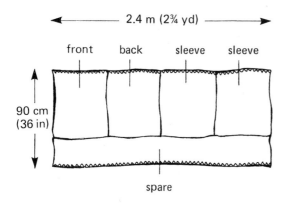

Diagram 87   *Cutting out the main part of the cowl neck top*

To cut the cowl collar, first cut a pattern. From the paper cut a rectangle 50 x 65 cm (20 x 26 in). Arrange this on the square of cheesecloth (diagram 88); it should just fit. Cut out carefully. The outside triangles are spare.

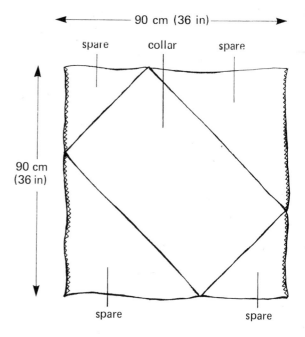

Diagram 88   *Cutting out the collar*

Making up   Join the shorter, shoulder edges of the back and front, leaving 30 cm (12 in) unstitched at the centre to form the neck opening. Press the seam open. On each sleeve, mark the centre of the shorter, shoulder edge and place it to the shoulder seam. Join using french seams. Starting with the wrong sides together, join the sleeve and side seams in one continuous french seam. Turn and stitch 2.5 cm (1 in) hems on the bottom and sleeve edges. Work your chosen decorative edging round these hems.

To make up the collar, join the shorter edges of the collar to make a tube. Turn a narrow hem on one edge. Work your chosen decorative edging. Join the remaining raw edge of the collar to the neck opening. Use a french seam, and start with the right side of the collar to the wrong side of the neck opening. Fold the collar in half, so that the edging shows and all the seams are hidden. Thread the elastic through the hems.

Adding a collar   You can add a cowl collar to the basic shirt, the long shirt and the shirt dress, and also to the bloused tunic top and the bloused dress. You will need to buy 90 cm (1 yd) extra cheesecloth. Follow the cutting out instructions given.

COWL NECK TOP WITH ADDED CUT OUT

COWL NECK TOP WITH PATCH POCKETS

Hooded Jacket

This long jacket has patch pockets, and makes a superb beach cover-up. It will fit up to 95 cm (38 in) bust, length 85 cm (34 in), sleeve seam 45 cm (18 in).

Materials
    2.9 m (3½ yd) cheesecloth
    thread to match
    thread to match or contrast for edging

Cutting out   Cut the cheesecloth across the width to give one piece, 60 x 90 cm (24 x 36 in) for the back, and two pieces, each 35 x 90 cm (14 x 36 in) for the front panels. Round off two corners of the back as shown (diagram 89). Round off one corner of each front, make sure that you have a left and right front. Cut a further piece, 40 x 90 cm (16 x 36 in) for the hood. From the selvedge of the remaining cheesecloth cut a 40 cm (16 in) strip. This is to be used for the pockets. Cut the last piece of cheesecloth in half to give two pieces, each 60 x 50 cm (23 x 20 in) for the sleeves. From spare fabric, cut two 32.5 cm (13 in) squares for the pockets. Round off one corner of each to match the fronts. Make sure that you have a left and a right pocket.

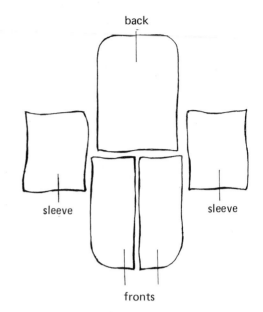

back

sleeve   sleeve

fronts

Diagram 90   *Arranging the pieces*

the shoulder seam. Put the wrong sides together, and join using a french seam (diagram 90). Press.

Fold the jacket in half, with wrong sides together. Work the first part of the french seam from the wrist edge of the sleeve and down the side of the main part, but leave 35 cm (14 in) unstitched at the centre to form the side slits (diagram 91).

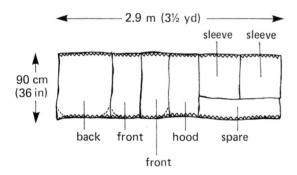

2.9 m (3½ yd)

90 cm
(36 in)

sleeve   sleeve

back   front   hood   spare

front

Diagram 89   *Cutting out the hooded jacket*

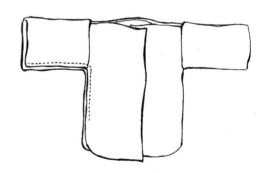

Diagram 91   *Sewing the side seam*

Making up   With right sides together, place the front on top of the back, making sure that the rounded corners match. Match the top edges; the fronts will overlap slightly. Work a 1.5 cm (⅝ in) flat seam across the shoulders leaving 30 cm (12 in) unstitched at the centre for the neck opening. Place the centre of the longer edge of the sleeve to

Fold the hood in half, matching the selvedges, with wrong sides facing. Stitch from the fold to the selvedges for the first part of the french seam. Turn and stitch the second part of the french seam. Join, using a french seam. Press the whole garment. Turn and tack narrow hems on the raw edges of the sleeves. Turn and tack narrow hems on the front

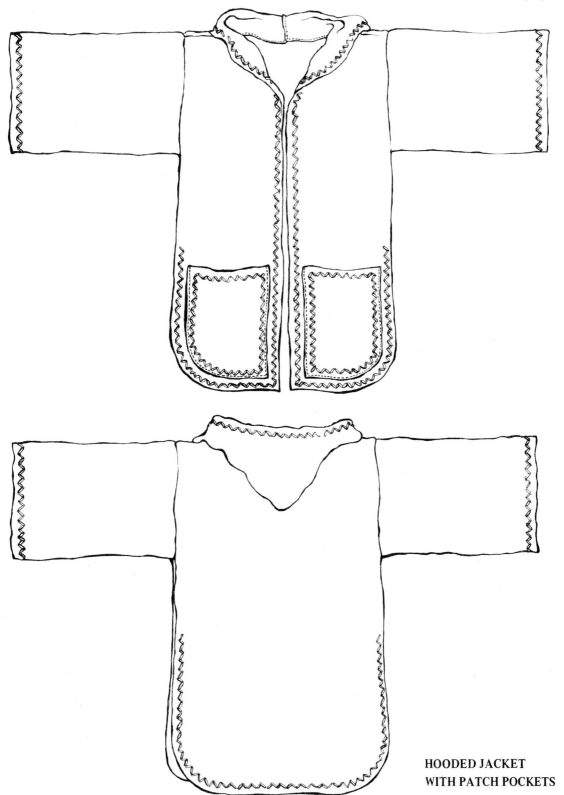

**HOODED JACKET
WITH PATCH POCKETS**

edges, bottom hem, side slits and hood opening. Stitch into place, using your chosen decorative edgings — you can sew the main part in one operation.

Turn and tack narrow hems on all the edges of the pockets; make sure you still have a matching pair. Stitch the hems into place using your chosen edging. Place the pockets just inside the edging on the fronts. Top stitch the pockets into place round three sides, leaving the top edge open so that you can put your hand in.

Patch Pockets

Adding patch pockets to even the simplest garment changes its character. Make pockets from any suitable sized square. Turn and stitch hems on all the edges. Pin the pocket to the garment, check that it looks right, move it if necessary, then top stitch it into place round three edges. Pockets can be made to match or contrast, and they can be decorated in many ways. Look through this book for ideas. Try stitching a pocket on the diagonal, or use triangular pockets. See also the pouch pocket on page 76.

DECORATIVE BRAIDS

There are many sorts of braid available, but some can be very expensive. With a little imagination, and some patience, you can produce your own colourful braid trims, at a fraction of the price, from seam tape or ric-rac braid.

Attaching Braid

Braid
If you intend to add only a small amount of trimming, or are decorating a small article, it is not too extravagant to use bought braid. Simply top stitch or oversew the braid into place. Make sure that you secure both edges.

Ric-rac braid
Ric-rac is easily available and reasonably cheap. It is distinctive in appearance, but can be made even more so with added embroidery. The simplest way of attaching ric-rac is to top stitch it straight down the centre. However, if stitched in this way the points tend to curl up after washing. A better way is to top stitch from point to point, although this takes longer to do (diagram 92).

The most attractive way of attaching ric-rac braid is to embroider it into place. It need not take much longer than top stitching. The simplest stitch to use is fly stitch. Tack the braid into position first, and then follow diagram 93.

Feather stitch is rather more difficult to do, but it is worthwhile practising to get it right (diagram 94).

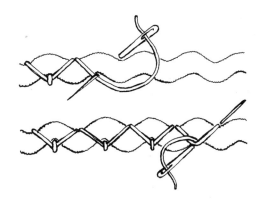

Diagram 93   *Fly stitching ric-rac braid*

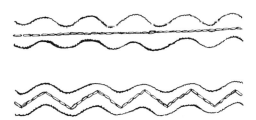

Diagram 92   *Top stitching ric-rac braid*

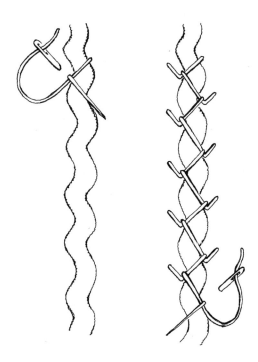

Diagram 94   *Feather stitching ric-rac braid*

Another attractive way of securing ric-rac braid is to use french knots (diagram 95).

Or you could use matching or contrasting thread to work a band of machine satin stitch (see page 65).

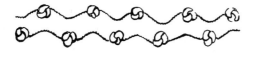

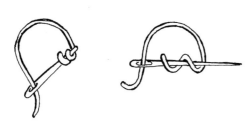

Diagram 95   *Attaching ric-rac braid with french knots*

Diagram 97   *Attaching straight tape with french knots*

Tapes

The straight tape intended to strengthen seams is the most useful type from which to make a decorative braid, but for straight rows of decoration bias binding can be used. This has the advantage of being available in several widths. Both straight tape and bias binding come in a wide range of colours.

Once again, the simplest way of attaching is top stitching. It is very effective if you use an open zigzag stitch in a contrasting colour (diagram 96).

If embroidering into place by hand you can use two rows of french knots (diagram 97). You could also use two rows of fly stitch (diagram 98).

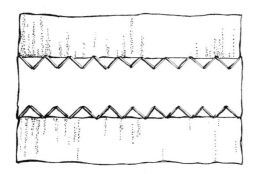

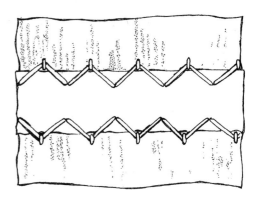

Diagram 96   *Zigzag machining straight tape*

Diagram 98   *Fly stitching straight tape*

If you have used top stitching to secure the tape, you can still add embroidery. Diagram 99 shows how to work continuous rows of cross stitch.

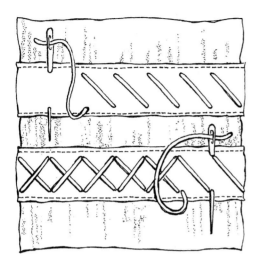

Diagram 99   *Adding cross stitch embroidery*

Another idea would be to add cross stitch stars. Diagram 100 shows how to work them.

If you are using wide bias binding you could add embroidered flowers, such as those given on page 82.

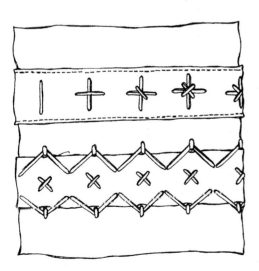

Diagram 100   *Making cross stitch stars*

Caftan

This is an ideal garment to lounge about in, or to use as a cover up. It will fit up to 95 cm (38 in) bust, very loosely, length 150 cm (58 in).

Materials
    3.5 m (3¾ yd) cheesecloth
    thread to match
    5 m (5½ yd) ric-rac braid
    5 m (5½ yd) straight tape (you could use bias
      binding)
    thread for top stitching or embroidery

Cutting out Across the width of the cheesecloth, cut four 7.5 cm (3 in) strips for the belt. Cut the remaining cheesecloth in half across the width to give two pieces, each 160 x 90 cm (62 x 36 in) for the back and front (diagram 101).
    From ric-rac braid, cut two 180 cm (72 in) lengths for the belt, and two 160 cm (62 in) lengths for the main part. Cut straight tape in the same way.

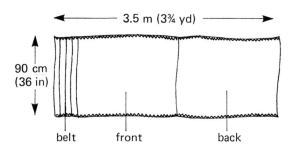

Diagram 101   *Cutting out the caftan*

Making up Make up the belt first. Join the short ends of the strips using a flat seam. Press. Fold the belt in half lengthways and press to mark the centre. Mark it with a line of tacking. Arrange the ric-rac braid on either side of this line, and tack then stitch into place. Arrange lengths of the seam tape outside the ric-rac braid making sure that you have left enough space at the top and bottom to work a 1.5 cm (⅝ in) flat seam. Stitch the tape into place.

Join the short ends of the second two strips.
    Place two completed strips together, with right sides facing. Work a 1.5 cm (⅝ in) flat seam on both long edges and one short end (diagram 102). Turn through as for rouleau. Press. Turn in the remaining raw edges and oversew them to neaten.

Diagram 102   *Making up the belt*

To make up the main part of the caftan, take the front and fold it so that the selvedges match. Press and tack to mark the centre. Arrange rows of trimming about 8 cm (3 in) on either side of this line. Stitch them into place.
    Place the back on top of the front, with right sides facing. Using a flat seam, join the shoulder edges, but leave 30 cm (12 in) unstitched at the centre to form the neck opening. Press the seam open along its entire length. Make the neck edges into hems and stitch them into place. Neaten the remaining shoulder seams. Join the side seams using a flat seam, but leave 30 cm (12 in) unstitched at the top for the armhole. Press the seams open. Neaten the armholes and side seams. To complete the caftan, fold and stitch a 10 cm (4 in hem on the bottom edge. All ends of the trimming should now be enclosed.

To adjust the length To lengthen or shorten the garment slightly, adjust the width of the lower hem. To lengthen considerably, work out how much longer you want your caftan to be, double this and buy this much more cheesecloth. To shorten, work out the adjustment, double this, and take this from the amount of fabric needed.
    Remember to adjust the amount of trimming you buy, too.

Adding extra braid You can add as many extra rows of ric-rac braid or straight tape as you fancy. You will need 1.8 m (2 yd) of braid for each two extra rows.

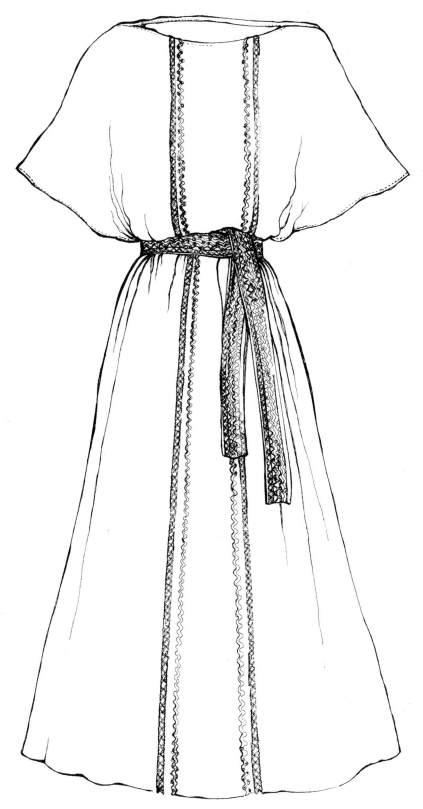

CAFTAN

Drawstring Top

This useful top has a pouch pocket and comes in two sizes to fit from a 80 cm (32 in) chest or bust to a 105 cm (42 in) chest or bust.

Large top

To fit up to 105 cm (42 in) chest or bust, length 65 cm (26 in), sleeve seam 50 cm (20 in).

Materials

    2.8 m (3⅜ yd) cheesecloth

    thread to match

    6.5 m (7 yd) straight tape or bias binding

    thread for top stitching or embroidery

Cutting out Cut the cheesecloth in half to give two pieces, each 140 x 90 cm (56 x 36 in).

From the selvedge of the first piece cut two 5 cm (2 in) strips for the bottom drawstrings. Cut the remaining cheesecloth in half to give two pieces, each 70 x 80 cm (28 x 32 in) for the back and front. The 70 cm (28 in) edge is the shoulder edge (diagram 103).

From the selvedges of the second piece, cut a 20 cm (8 in) strip. This is spare, and will be used to make the pouch pocket. Next cut a 5 cm (2 in) strip, and cut this in half to make two wrist drawstrings, each 70 cm (28 in) long. Cut the remaining cheesecloth in half to give two pieces, each 70 x 65 cm (28 x 26 in) for the sleeves. The 70 cm (28 in) edge is the shoulder edge.

Following diagram 105, cut a paper pattern for the pocket. Pin it onto the spare cheesecloth, and cut out.

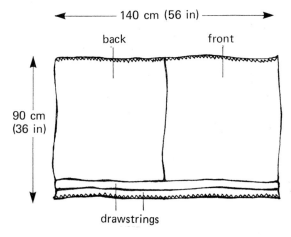

Diagram 103   *Cutting out the large drawstring top (first length)*

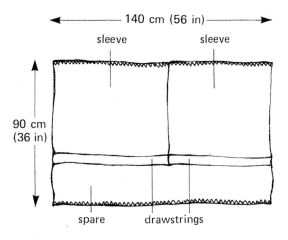

Diagram 104   *Cutting out the large drawstring top (second length)*

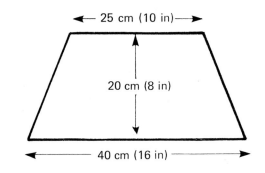

Diagram 105   *The pouch pocket*

Making up Turn and stitch narrow hems on all the edges of the pocket. Tack tape just inside the hems on the right side, and stitch into place. Fold the front in half, and press to mark the centre. Mark it with a line of tacking. In the same way, mark and tack 15 cm (6 in), 20 cm (8 in) and 25 cm (10 in) on either side of the centre line. Use this tacking as a guide whilst arranging the six rows of seam tape. Stitch the tape into place, then remove the tacking.

With the right sides together, join the shoulder edges of the back and front, leaving 35 cm (14 in) unstitched at the centre for the neck opening. Neaten. On the sleeves mark the centre of the shoulder edge, and place it to the shoulder seam. Join using french seams. Press. Starting with the wrong sides together, join the sleeve and side seams in one continuous french seam. Turn and stitch 5 cm (2 in) hems on the sleeve and bottom edges.

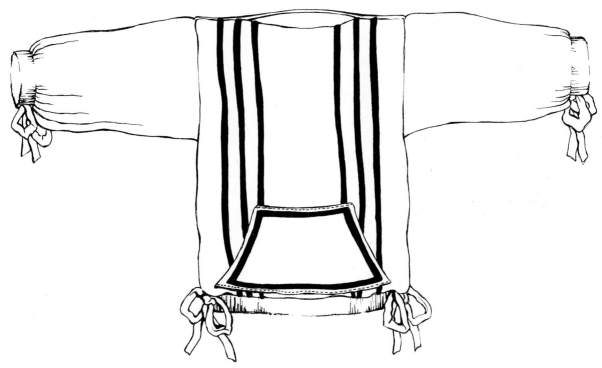

DRAWSTRING TOP WITH POUCH POCKET

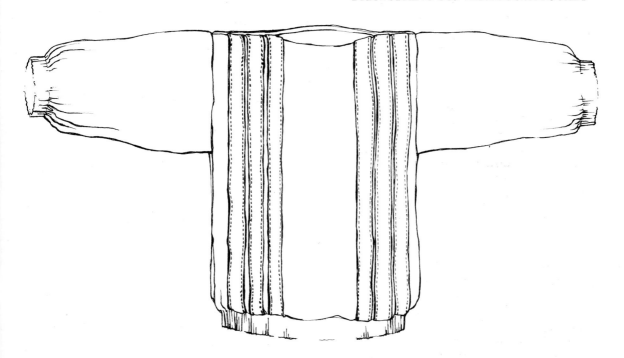

TOP WITH ELASTICATED CUFFS AND WELT

Make openings for the drawstrings at the side and sleeve seams. Carefully snip through the stitching on the outside only. Oversew the edges to form a slit. Add extra stitches at the top and bottom so that there is no chance of the rest of the seam coming undone. Make the drawstrings into rouleaux, neaten the ends and thread them through the hems to emerge at the slits. Use a safety pin or bodkin attached to the end to help you.

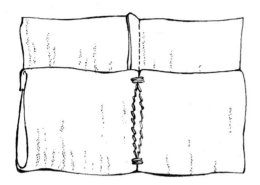

Diagram 106   *Making the side slits*

Try on the shirt, and position the pocket centrally on the front, just above the bottom hem. It should not lie flat, or you will not be able to put your hands in it. Pin it into place. Take the shirt off and top stitch the pocket into place, stitching along the top and bottom edges only.

To adjust the length   To lengthen slightly, make the hems narrower, but make sure they are at least 2.5 cm (1 in) wide or you will not be able to thread the drawstrings through. To make a larger adjustment, do not cut the drawstrings from cheesecloth but use elastic. To shorten slightly, adjust the width of the hem, or cut some fabric from the bottom edge of the back, front and sleeves.

Medium top

This size will fit up to 95 cm (38 in) bust or chest, length 65 cm (26 in), sleeve seam 50 cm (20 in).

Materials
   2.4 m (2¾ yd) cheesecloth
   6.5 m (7 yd) straight tape or bias binding
   thread to match
   thread for embroidery

Cutting out   Cut the cheesecloth in half to give two pieces, each 120 x 90 cm (48 x 36 in). From the first piece of cheesecloth, cut two 5 cm (2 in) strips for the bottom drawstrings, each 120 cm (48 in) long. Cut the remaining cheesecloth in half to give two pieces, each 60 x 80 cm (24 x 32 in) for the back and front (diagram 107). The 60 cm (24 in) edge is the shoulder edge.

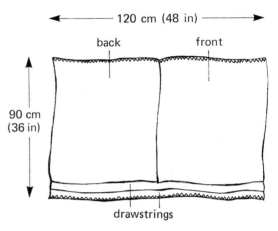

Diagram 107   *Cutting out the medium drawstring top (first length)*

From the second piece, cut a 20 cm (8 in) strip. This is spare, and will be used for the pouch pocket. Then cut a 5 cm (2 in) strip; cut this in half to give two wrist ties, each 60 cm (24 in) long. Cut the remaining fabric in half to give two pieces, each 60 x 65 cm (24 x 26 in) for the sleeves. The 60 cm (24 in) edge is the shoulder edge. Cut the pocket as for the large shirt.

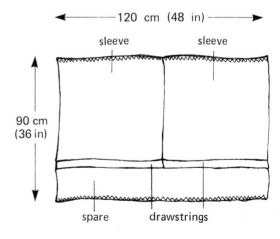

Diagram 108   *Cutting out the medium drawstring top (second length)*

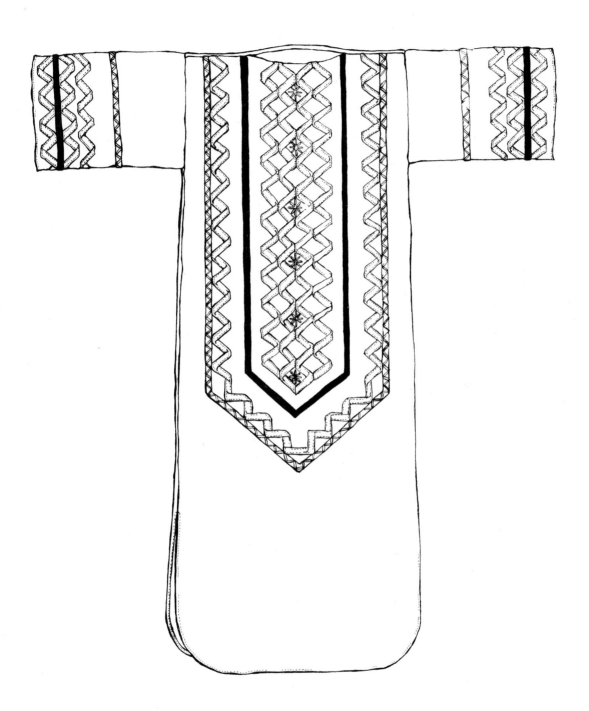

**SHIRT DRESS WITH ADDED BRAID
DECORATION**

Making up   Make up as for the large shirt, but leave 30 cm (12 in) unstitched for the neck opening, and making the lines of tacking 10 cm (4 in), 15 cm (6 in) and 20 cm (8 in) on either side of the centre.

To adjust the length   Adjust as for the large shirt.

To add decoration   If you are using straight tape you can fold it backwards and forwards on itself to form zigzags (diagram 109). This is not possible with bias binding. If this is to be effective it must be even. To help you keep it even, mark guidelines with tacking first. The zigzags can be arranged to form waves (diagram 110) or diamonds (diagram 111). If you arrange the tape in zigzags to form diamonds, you could embroider flowers or some other motif inside.

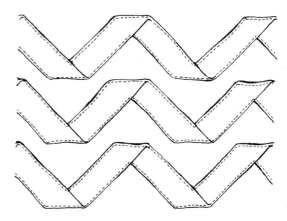

Diagram 110   *Attaching the seam tape with waves*

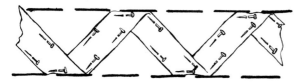

Diagram 109   *Attaching the seam tape with zigzags*

Braid decoration can be added to many garments in this book. The dress on page 79 is the shirt dress from an earlier section (you will find instructions on page 34). The rows of tape were sewn into place before joining the pieces together — so no tape ends show.

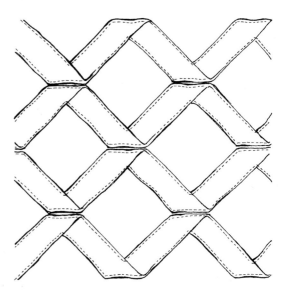

Diagram 111   *Attaching the seam tape with diamonds*

EMBROIDERY

Even the simplest embroidery adds a hint of luxury to clothes, no matter how plain the basic garment.

Hand Embroidery

Equipment
    embroidery pencil or dressmaker's carbon
    embroidery thread
    crewel needles
    embroidery hoop

Do not choose too thick an embroidery thread, it will look clumsy. Whatever thread you choose, make sure that the eye of the needle is the right size. If the eye is too small, it will be difficult to thread, and when you have managed to thread the needle you will find that the eye frays the thread as you work, so that it soon looks worn. Too large an eye, and the needle will continually unthread itself, which is extremely irritating.

Method
Cut a length of thread which just reaches from your fingers to your elbow. It is not worth trying to use a longer length, as the thread snaps and tangles. Transfer the design onto the fabric, then, making sure that the design will appear in the centre, put the cheesecloth into the embroidery hoop. Pull the fabric taut and tighten the outer hoop if possible. Embroider over the lines of the design. Make sure that the stitches completely cover the lines of the design as dressmaker's carbon or embroidery pencil does not always wash out.

For linear design use stem stitch or chain stitch. Diagrams 112 and 113 show how to work these stitches. Practise on oddments of cheesecloth until you gain confidence.

A range of simple flowers can be easily embroidered by hand. They are extremely effective and can be used in many different ways. Since cheesecloth is loosely woven you can make pierced flowers.

Push a knitting needle through the fabric, and move it backwards and forwards to enlarge the hole. Then embroider round the edges with buttonhole stitch as shown (diagram 114). To make an open centre for any of the flowers that follow, pierce the hole and oversew the edges, then work further embroidery.

Diagram 112   *Stem stitch*

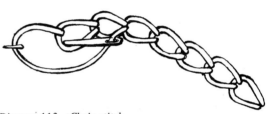

Diagram 113   *Chain stitch*

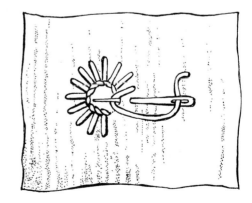

Diagram 114   *Pierced flower*

Straight stitch daisies can be made in a variety of sizes (diagram 115). Add extra colour by filling the centre of the daisies with french knots worked in a contrasting thread. See page 72 for how to work french knots. These could also be used to make small flowers (diagram 116).

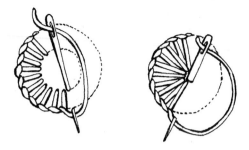

Diagram 117 *Buttonhole flowers with open and closed centres*

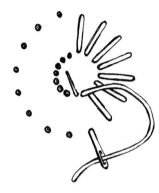

Diagram 115 *Straight stitch daisy*

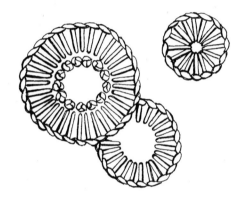

Diagram 118 *Buttonhole flowers and french knots*

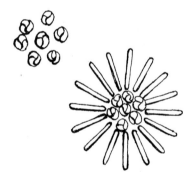

Diagram 116 *Making the centres with french knots*

Buttonhole flowers are also easy to work. They can be made with an open or closed centre (diagram 117). Draw circles as guidelines, using coins as templates. Once again, you can use french knots to add interest (diagram 118).

For a more open flower, space out the stitches (diagram 119). This flower is a little more difficult to do than the closed buttonhole flower, as the stitches tend to slant the wrong way unless you take extra care.

Diagram 119 *Buttonhole flowers using open stitching*

Lazy daisy stitch is simply another name for chain stitch worked singly (diagram 120). Use the stitches singly to embroider leaves or buds, or group the stitches together in various ways to produce a variety of flowers (diagram 121).

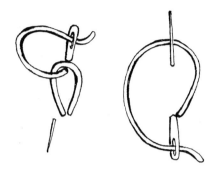

Diagram 120   *Lazy daisy stitch*

Diagram 121   *Lazy daisy stitch forming flowers, buds and leaves*

Machine Embroidery

Machine satin stitch is quick and easy to work but is not so adaptable as hand embroidery.

Equipment
    embroidery pencil or dressmaker's carbon
    thread for embroidery
    embroidery hoop
    swing needle sewing machine
You can use ordinary sewing cotton or special machine embroidery thread. This method uses more thread than you expect.

Method
Transfer your design onto the cheesecloth using the embroidery pencil or dressmaker's carbon. Thread and adjust the machine as for machine edging (see page 65). However, as you are sewing a single thickness of cheesecloth and not a folded hem, you will have to hold the material taut so that the embroidery does not pucker. Use your embroidery hoop to do this. Place the cheesecloth over the outer hoop. Make sure that it is right side up, and that the design is in the centre of the hoop. Place the inner ring on top, and push it into place. The fabric is now at the bottom of the hoop, not at the top as for hand embroidery. Stitch over the lines of the design. You will find that the cheesecloth moves quite slowly, and it is therefore easy to keep to the lines of the design. If you alter the swing of the needles as you sew, you can produce graduated bands of embroidery. Practise on a spare piece of cheesecloth until you have gained confidence.

Machine embroidery of this kind is not suitable for small flowers. You can combine hand and machine embroidery, working the stems and other lines by machine and the flowers by hand, or you can cut flower shapes from mounted cheesecloth and stitch these into place (see pages 58 and 90 for flower patterns, and page 57 for the technique).

Long Jacket

This lightweight, comfortable jacket will look superb worn over the other clothes in this book, and will fit up to 90 cm (36 in) bust loosely, length 85 cm (34 in), sleeve seam 45 cm (18 in).

Materials

    2.5 m (3 yd) cheesecloth
    thread to match
    thread to match or contrast for edging
    thread to match or contrast for embroidery

Cutting out   Cut the cheesecloth across the width to give one piece 60 x 90 cm (24 x 36 in) for the back, and two pieces, each 35 x 90 cm (14 x 36 in) for the front panels (diagram 122). Round off the corners of the front panels as shown. Make sure that you have a left and a right front. From the selvedges of the remaining cheesecloth, cut a 40 cm (16 in) strip. This will be used for the ties. Cut the last piece of cheesecloth in half to give two pieces, each 60 x 50 cm (23 x 20 in), for the sleeves.

From the spare cheesecloth, cut two 5 cm (2 in) strips for the ties. You could use the remainder of the fabric to make patch pockets, and embroider them to match the lapels.

Making up   With right sides together, place the front panels on top of the back, making sure that the rounded edges of the front panels are to the centre (diagram 123). Match the top edges; the front panels will overlap slightly. Work a 1.5 cm (⅝ in) flat seam across the shoulders, leaving 30 cm (12 in) unstitched at the centre for the neck opening. Press the seam open along its entire length. Turn and tack a narrow hem to neaten the back of the neck. Place the centre of the longer edge of the sleeve to the shoulder seam. Put the wrong sides together, and stitch them into place using french seams. Press.

    Fold the jacket in half, with wrong sides together. Work the first part of the french seam from the wrist edge of the sleeve to the hem of the main part (diagram 124). Work the second side of the jacket in the same way. Turn the jacket inside out (the right sides will now be facing), and complete the

LONG JACKET

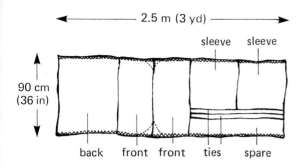

Diagram 122   *Cutting out the long jacket*

french seams. Press. Turn and tack narrow hems on the raw edges of the sleeves. Turn and tack narrow hems on the front and bottom edges, including the curved corners. Stitch the hems into place, using shell edging (see page 65). Make the ties into rouleaux, and neaten the ends. Fold the top corners of the front foward to form the collar. Press. Attach the ties at this point.

Trace diagram 125 and transfer it (using dressmaker's carbon) to the right side of the collar. Embroider over the lines of the design using hand embroidery or machine satin stitch. If embroidering by hand, you could fill the centre of the flower with french knots.

To adjust the length   This jacket cannot be made any longer. To shorten, cut the required amount from the bottom edge of the back, front panels and sleeves. Remember to adjust the curved front edges also.

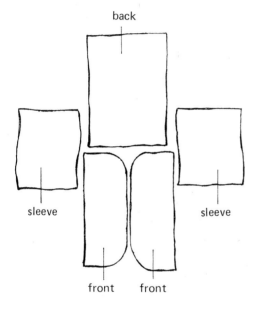

Diagram 123   *Arranging the pieces*

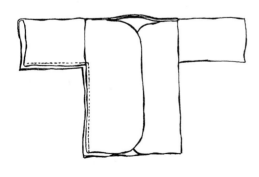

Diagram 124   *Sewing the side seam*

Diagram 125   *Design for embroidery*

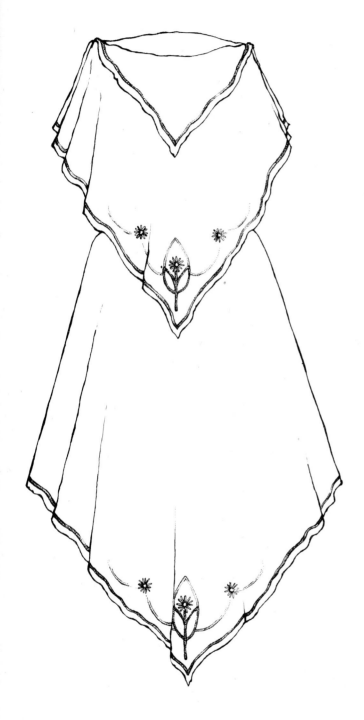

TOP, SKIRT AND SCARF

Skirt, Top And Scarf Set

This fashionable threesome will add a sparkle of life to your wardrobe. The triangular skirt and top will fit up to 95 cm (38 in) bust, and 100 cm (40 in) hip. The length of the top is 65 cm (26 in) at its longest point, and the skirt 95 cm (38 in) at its longest point. The matching scarf, which can be worn round your hair, neck or waist, depending on your mood, is approximately 120 x 30 cm (48 x 12 in) long.

Materials

    3 m (3⅜ yd) cheesecloth
    thread to match
    shirring elastic
    thread to match or contrast for shirring
    thread to match or contrast for embroidery

Cutting out Across the width of the cheesecloth cut two pieces, each 90 cm (36 in) square. Mark one corner; from this point measure and mark 40 cm (16 in) along the edge. Do the same on the adjoining edge. Join these marks and cut off the corner. This is the waist edge. Cut the second square to match. These are the back and front of the skirt. From the selvedge of the remaining cheesecloth cut a 30 cm (12 in) strip. This piece, which should be 120 x 30 cm (48 x 12 in), is for the scarf. Cut the last piece of fabric in half to give two pieces, each 60 cm (24 in) square. These are the back and front of the top.

Making up Turn and stitch narrow hems on all four edges of the scarf. Machine satin stitch can be used to secure the hems. Trace the design from diagram 127 and transfer it to the cheesecloth.

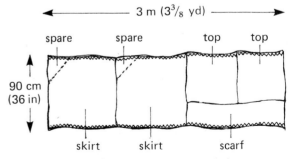

Diagram 126 *Cutting out the adult skirt, top and scarf*

Position it at the centre of each short side.

Use the edge of a saucer as a guide for marking the scallops. Embroider over the lines of the design. Then embroider or attach your chosen flower; you can add extra flowers at the points of the scallops.

Place the front of the skirt on top of the back, with wrong sides facing, then work french seams as shown (diagram 128). Turn and stitch narrow hems on the bottom and waist edges; you can use machine satin stitch for this. Work three rows of shirring close to the waist edge. Transfer the design and work the embroidery as for the scarf.

Turn and stitch narrow hems on all edges of the back and front of the triangular top. You can use machine satin stitch again (diagram 129). Place the front on top of the back, with wrong sides facing. As when cutting out the skirt, mark 20 cm (8 in) on each side of one corner — but do not cut off. Oversew the front and back together for 5 cm (2 in). Fold the corner forward. Transfer the design to this corner, and complete the embroidery. Repeat the design and scallops on the bottom corner. Work the back in the same way. Try on the top and pin the back and front together at the underarm. Make sure you can still move your arms freely. Stitch firmly just at these points.

To adjust the length   To lengthen the top slightly, fold less cheesecloth forward, but be careful — if you make the flap too small you will not be able to get the top over your head, nor will you have sufficient room for the embroidery. Similarly, to lengthen the skirt slightly, cut less off the waist edge, but check that you can still get the skirt on and off. To shorten the top or skirt, tack the garment together and try it on, then trim the required amount from the bottom edge.

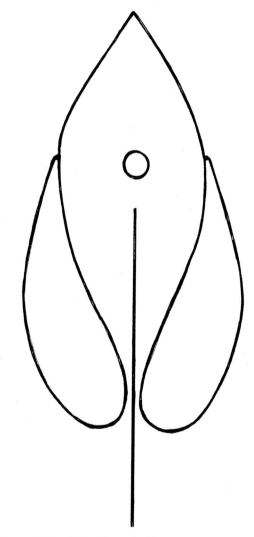

Diagram 127   *Design for embroidery*

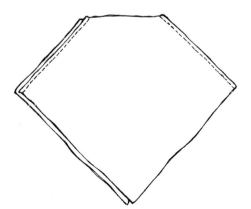

Diagram 128   *Making the skirt side seams*

Diagram 129   *Making the shoulder seams*

Matching Top And Scarf

This pretty top will fit up to 95 cm (38 in) bust; its length at the longest point is 65 cm (26 in). The matching scarf is approximately 120 x 30 cm (48 x 12 in) long.

Materials
    1.2 m (1⅜ yd) cheesecloth
    thread to match
    thread to match or contrast for embroidery

Cutting out   From the selvedge of the cheesecloth cut a 30 cm (12 in) strip. This is for the scarf. Cut the remaining fabric in half to give two pieces, each 60 cm (24 in) square. These are for the back and the front.

Making up   Make up in the same way as described above.

Triangular Skirt

This will fit up to 100 cm (40 in) hips; its length at the longest point is 95 cm (38 in).

Materials
    1.8 m (2 yd) cheesecloth
    thread to match
    shirring elastic
    thread to match or contrast for shirring
    thread to match or contrast for embroidery

Cutting out   Cut the cheesecloth in half to give two pieces, each 90 cm (36 in) square. Mark one corner; from this point measure and mark 40 cm (16 in) along the edge. Do the same on the adjoining edge. Join these marks and cut off the corner.

Making up   Make up in the same way as described above.

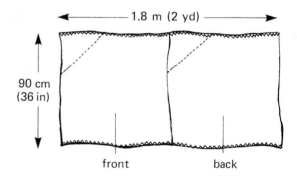

Diagram 131   *Cutting out the skirt*

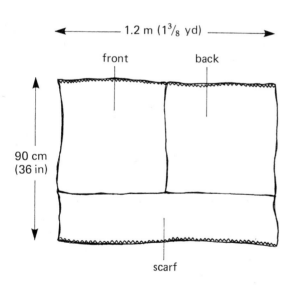

Diagram 130   *Cutting out the scarf and top*

Child's Scarf, Top And Skirt

This appealing child's version of the triangular outfit will fit up to 75 cm (30 in) chest, and 80 cm (32 in) hip. The length of the top is 45 cm (18 in) at its longest point, and the skirt 65 cm (26 in) at its longest point. The matching scarf is approximately 120 x 30 cm (48 x 12 in) long.

Materials
    1.65 m (1⅝ yd) cheesecloth
    thread to match
    shirring elastic
    thread to match or contrast for shirring
    thread to match or contrast for embroidery

Cutting out Across the width of the cheesecloth cut a 45 cm (18 in) strip. Cut this in half to give two pieces, each 45 cm (18 in) square. These are the back and front of the top. From the selvedge of the remaining cheesecloth, cut a 30 cm (12 in) strip. This is the scarf (diagram 132).

    Cut the last piece of cheesecloth in half to give two pieces, each 60 cm (24 in) square. Mark one corner, and from this point measure and mark 25 cm (10 in) along the edge. Do the same on the adjoining edge. Join these marks, and cut off the corner.

Making up Make up following the instructions given for the adult's version. On the top, mark 15 cm (6 in) in from the corner for the start of the shoulder seam. You will find that the design does not fit this corner when folded forward, so use scallops and small flowers instead.

Adding Embroidery

Embroidery can be added to most of the garments in this book. It can be added to pockets made from spare fabric — complete the embroidery before attaching the pocket to the garment. Squares, rectangles or triangles of spare cheesecloth can also be hemmed and have embroidery added to make scarves; gold metal sequins can also be sewn to the edge of the scarf for the 'Greek' or 'gipsy' look.

Designing Embroidery

It is very easy to design your own embroidery. Look through books and magazines to find a design that appeals to you. Children's books are a good source of simple shapes that are easy to copy. You will find that linear designs are the easiest to work — and the most effective. Broderie anglaise is a good source of designs for pierced embroidery. Link the flowers or holes with stem stitch. If you cannot find or create any suitable designs of your own, you can buy commercial embroidery transfers from a haberdashery shop, which can be applied to the fabric by means of a hot iron.

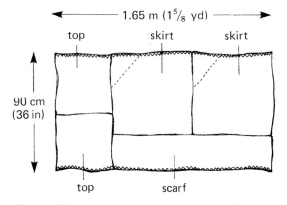

Diagram 132 *Cutting out the child's skirt, scarf and top*

MULTI-TECHNIQUE

Each section of this book has been devoted to a particular technique, and this final chapter shows how the various techniques can be combined. This results in the most individual and original clothes — clothes which are, in fact, unique.

Wedding Dress

Following the dictum — 'something old, something new, something borrowed, something blue' — this wedding dress can be shirred and edged in baby blue. Blue cheesecloth can also be used to make the cut out flowers and a blue garter. The bride can wear cut out flowers in her hair, and a shawl trimmed to match the dress. It will fit up to 95 cm (38 in) bust, length 120 cm (46 in).

Materials
6 m (7 yd) cheesecloth for main part and frills
20 cm (¼ yd) cheesecloth for flowers and garter
oddments of iron-on interlining
thread to match
shirring elastic
thread for shirring to match or contrast
thread for edging to match or contrast

Cutting out Cut a section 350 x 90 cm (144 x 36 in) for the main part, and 250 x 90 cm (108 x 36 in) for the frills. From the cheesecloth for the main part, cut two 20 cm (8 in) strips for the top, and three pieces, each 110 x 90 cm (42 x 36 in), for the skirt (diagram 133).

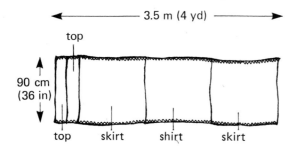

Diagram 133   *Cutting out the main part and top*

From the cheesecloth for the frills cut twenty-five 10 cm (4 in) strips (diagram 134).

From the final piece of cheesecloth cut a 7.5 cm (3 in) strip for the garter. Mount the remaining cheesecloth on the interlining to make cut out flowers.

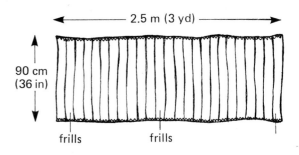

Diagram 134   *Cutting out the frills*

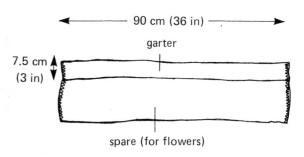

Diagram 135   *Cutting out the garter and flowers*

Diagram 136
Pattern for flower cut outs

WEDDING DRESS

Trace the flower shape in diagram 136, and use it as a pattern for cutting out as many flowers as possible. For alternative flower shapes see page 58.

Making up   Place the two strips for the top right sides together. Stitch flat seams on both the selvedge edges. Press the seams open. Turn and stitch a 1.5 cm (⅝ in) hem on one raw edge. Stitch six rows of shirring 2.5 cm (1 in) apart. Make sure that the first row goes through all three layers of the top hem.

Take three pieces of cheesecloth for the skirt. Place two pieces together, with right sides facing. Work a flat seam on the selvedge edge. Press the seam open. With right sides facing, stitch a flat seam to join to one selvedge of the third skirt piece. Press the seam open. Join the remaining selvedges (diagram 137). Gather one raw edge of the skirt and attach it to the remaining raw edge of the top. Turn and stitch a 5 cm (2 in) hem on the remaining raw edge of the skirt.

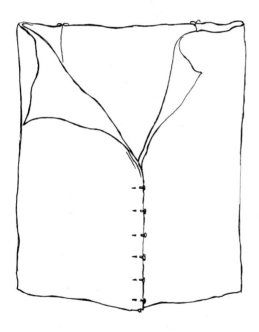

Diagram 137   *Making up the skirt*

Take five of the frill strips, and join the short ends together to make one circular frill. Pin and tack narrow hems on both the raw edges. Complete a further four frills in the same way. Stitch the hems using your chosen edging stitch.

For a rather more conventional bride's dress, shell tucking in white is delightful (or for a party dress try red machine satin stitch on black cheesecloth).

On the skirt, mark the position for the first frill, level with the top fold of the hem. Mark the position of the second frill 15 cm (6in) above this, and a further three frills the same distance apart. Stitch the frills into place. Arrange the cut out flowers as desired, and stitch them into place. You could use beads for this, especially large pearls, or stitch on silver sequins to outline the flowers, or use beads to fill the centres.

To adjust the length   To lengthen or shorten slightly, adjust the bottom hem. To lengthen considerably, work out the adjustment, treble it, and add this amount to the fabric needed for the main part. To shorten, take this amount away from the fabric needed.

Adding decoration   Depending on the type of cheesecloth you select and the stitches you use, this dress can look sweet and demure — all in white as a traditional bride's dress — or dark and sultry — gipsy-like in black, with bold edging and multi-coloured flowers with beaded centres.

Garter

Join the shorter edges of the cheesecloth using a flat seam. Turn and tack narrow hems on both the raw edges. Use your chosen edging stitch to secure the hems. Work two rows of shirring down the centre. Fasten off securely, to ensure a firm fit above the knee. Add flowers for decoration.

GARTER

Bridesmaid's Dress

This delightful child's dress can be trimmed to match the bridal gown. It will fit up to 75 cm (30 in) chest, length 95 cm (38 in).

Materials

    3.6 m (4 yd) cheesecloth for main part and frills
    oddments of iron-on interlining
    thread to match
    shirring elastic
    thread to match or contrast for shirring
    thread to match or contrast for edging

Cutting out   From the cheesecloth cut nine 10 cm (4 in) strips for the frills, and two 15 cm (6 in) strips. Cut 30 cm (12 in) from the selvedge of each to give two pieces, each 60 x 15 cm (24 x 6 in) for the top. The remaining piece of cheesecloth, 240 x 90 cm (96 x 36 in), is for the skirt (diagram 138). Mount the spare pieces of cheesecloth onto the interlining. Cut out the flowers as for the wedding dress.

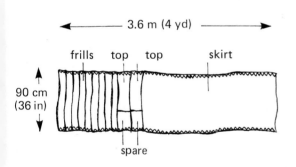

Diagram 138   *Cutting out the bridesmaid's dress*

Making up   Make up as for the wedding dress. You will not have to join the skirt pieces together. Join three strips together to form each frill.

To adjust the length   To lengthen or shorten slightly, change the width of the bottom hem. To shorten considerably, cut the desired amount from the selvedge edge of the skirt before making up.

Toddler's Dress

To complete the wedding ensemble — or as a party dress for the young sophisticate — this frilly dress will appeal to the very youngest of the family. It will fit 50 cm (20 in) chest, length 65 cm (26 in).

Materials

    1.5 m (1¾ yd) cheesecloth
    thread to match
    shirring elastic
    thread to match or contrast for shirring
    thread to match or contrast for edging

Cutting out   From the selvedge cut two 10 cm (4 in) strips for the frill. The remaining 150 x 70 cm (63 x 28 in) is for the main part (diagram 139).

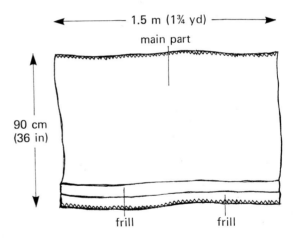

Diagram 139   *Cutting out the toddler's frilled dress*

Making up   Join the shorter edges of the main part. Turn a narrow hem at the top, and work three rows of shirring. Turn and stitch a 2.5 cm (1 in) hem at the bottom edge. Join the frill and edge. Attach 7.5 cm (3 in) from the bottom edge. Add some flowers left over from the other dresses, or cut a section from the frill (before you make it up) and use this to make mounted cut out flowers.

Further Ideas

No, I have not forgotten the page boy. Why not adapt the long shirt, edge it to match the dresses, and add a tie belt so that it looks like a cossack tunic. Last but not least (in fact, essential!) the groom — but I am sure that you have your own ideas, adding frills to a basic shirt perhaps, to make the groom's outfit match that of the bride.

Having read through this book, you should now be able to make a range of simple garments to provide a basic wardrobe for yourself or your children, and be ready to apply some of the techniques you have mastered. If you now look back to earlier chapters, you will see further possibilities for added decoration, perhaps using a combination of techniques. For example, on the shirt dress on page 34, use shirring to replace the tie belt and add patch pockets (see page 70) and a cowl collar (see page 66), decorated with embroidery, cut outs or ric-rac braid to produce a very different, softly feminine dress. To reverse the process, make up the long jacket on page 84 in a bright colour, omit the embroidery, and decorate it using wide bias binding and contrast top stitching.

You will also find it easy to interchange embroidery designs with each other and with mounted cut outs, to add them to other articles in the book, or even to ready-made cheesecloth garments.

If you feel you want to revitalize your wardrobe — you want something new — you can use the techniques shown in this book to completely change the look of an existing garment — by dyeing, by adding frills, or simply by working an edging stitch over the existing hems. You can also cut a completely new top from an old skirt, or a child's shirt from an adult's. The ideas shown here offer many short cuts to save unnecessary time and effort, and make dressmaking a pleasure rather than a task.

I hope you are beginning to see the endless possibilities afforded by the items and techniques shown in this book, and discover how easy it is to produce truly individual clothes with just a little ingenuity and imagination.

INDEX